acknowledgements

This workbook has been developed to assist people in their recovei emotional, and spiritual wounds of codependence. This work focuses on the five core life skills that are difficult for people with codependence: (1) esteeming oneself from within; (2) establishing and maintaining functional boundaries; (3) owning one's reality; (4) identifying and meeting one's needs; and (5) living in moderation.

This book originated in 2003 as a lecture/presentation series for the Codependence Recovery Program at Life Healing Center of Santa Fe. In 2013 Focus Healthcare of CA asked me to revise and expand this material into a book and generously funded its editing, design, and publication.

This book was designed as a resource for both individual study and facilitated group workshops. It offers the reader both a working understanding of codependence issues and practical skills to heal the wounds of codependence.

This book is about our human self working in partnership with our soul. I invite you to explore the hypothesis that we are both human and divine. My perspective is that our lack of conscious connection with our soul leads to codependence. Thus healing the wounds of codependence will also assist our human self to begin living in alignment with our soul. For more information on Living in Alignment, please explore www.LivingInAlignment.ca.

I am indebted to Pia Mellody of The Meadows (where I was an intern) and a number of other practitioners in the codependence recovery field for many of the insights compiled and distilled into this workbook. I acknowledge and credit the following people for their pioneering contributions to the field that I have built on and adapted for the wisdom in this book.

Pia Mellody	Janet G. Woititz	Authur Diekman	Ronald and Patricia Potter-Efron
Robert Burney	Riane Eisler	Penny Pierce	Karol Truman and Jon Kabat-Zinn
Melody Beattie	Jacquelin Small	Arnold Mindell	Barry and Janae Weinhold
	Claudia Black	Anne Wilson Schaef	

A special Thank You goes to Mark Lersch for his editorial, graphic, and technical assistance in preparing the lecture series, and to Wayne Marshall Jones for his copyediting, proofreading, graphic design, and consulting work on this publication. His dedication and steadfast attention to detail have been invaluable in preparing this revised and expanded workbook.

I am grateful for the support of the late Marty McEvoy of Life Healing Center and Becky Johnson and Liz Cervio of Focus Healthcare CA. I would also like to thank my clients for the opportunity to be their teacher and they mine. Last, but certainly not least, I express my gratitude for the guidance that has continuously been offered from Source energy.

—Darcy S. Clarke MA, LPCC, CADC-II, CTPC

The CreateSpace Edition is Printed in USA

ISBN: 978-0-9917101-4-0

a psychospiritual model of recovery from codependence

Qualities inherent in humanity	Causes of ego wounding*	Primary patterns of codependence	Maladaptive coping styles	Relational problems (self & others)	The recovery process
1 I am Valuable	Insufficient nurturing around my inherent worth	Difficulty esteeming myself from within	Less than vs. better than	Esteem issues	Learning to love myself
2 I am Vulnerable	Insufficient nurturing around protecting myself	Difficulty establishing & maintaining healthy boundaries	Too vulnerable vs. invulnerable	Enmeshment & avoidance issues	Learning to protect myself
3 I am Imperfect	Insufficient nurturing around acceptance of my humanness	Difficulty owning my reality	Bad/rebellious vs. good/perfect	Dishonesty issues (not speaking my truth)	Learning to develop self-awareness
4 I am Interdependent	Insufficient nurturing around my connectedness	Difficulty identifying & meeting my needs	Dependent vs. anti-dependent	Inter-connectedness issues	Learning to care for myself
5 I am Spontaneous	Insufficient nurturing around containing myself	Difficulty expressing myself appropriately	Out of control vs. overcontrolling	Power issues	Learning to live in moderation

* Adapted from Pia Mellody's model of Codependence

table of contents

codependence group guidelines

1. What you see and hear in the group stays in the group.
2. Be clear and concise. Speak your truth.
3. Express one thought, opinion, observation, etc. at a time.
4. Speak from your own experience. Avoid giving advice.
5. Use 'I' statements.
6. Offer feedback only when asked.
7. Be punctual.
8. Be willing to 'sit' with your discomfort. Do not leave the room.
9. Be willing to participate. Speak and listen actively.
10. Encourage yourself to be vulnerable in the group.
11. Listen with honor, allowing others to finish speaking.
12. Take responsibility for your experience.

5 practices to codependence recovery

	My Life Skills	My Group Skills
1	Practice loving myself.	Affirm my birthright to be here.
2	Practice establishing / maintaining functional boundaries.	Utilize my listening / talking boundaries.
3	Practice identifying & owning what I think / feel / experience in the moment.	Speak my truth to myself and others.
4	Practice identifying my needs and nurturing myself.	Ask myself compassionately, 'What do I need right now?'
5	Practice living in moderation.	Monitor how much I speak and what I am saying.

practice, practice, practice, practice, practice!

1. experiencing authentic living
a program to awaken your human self

If you bring forth what is within you,
what you bring forth will save you.
If you don't bring forth what is within you,
what you don't bring forth will destroy you.
—Jesus in *The Gospel According to Thomas*

I. a psychospiritual model of healing

◆ This program was developed to help you discover an **authentic sense of all that you are**. You will explore your humanness from the perspective of your deep (often unconscious) experience of the Mysterious that many traditions have called your soul, using **a psychospiritual model of recovery** that taps into your soul's wisdom.

◆ This approach will assist your human self to **experience a conscious union** with your deepest self, with others, with all life forms, with a higher Power, and with living your life. It is a synthesis of the work of many people involved in the consciousness movement across Planet Earth.

◆ This program will facilitate **aligning your human self with your soul**, allowing your human self to assume its rightful position as the agent/artist of your soul. This transformational process involves letting go of **self-defeating patterns** and discovering **soul fulfillment**.

◆ Until your alignment with your soul is secure, your mind will continually **interrupt** your recovery process with its **unhealed wounding**. As a result you **identify with your ego's demands** and abandon your connection with your soul, leading to codependence (a futile attempt to fill your emptiness).

◆ A major focus of this psychospiritual recovery program is **recovering from codependence.** The recovery process will help you get your insecurities (fears) out of the driver's seat and discover how to align your human self with your soul.

◆ This recovery program fosters **life skills to become a healthy human being**. It will address your unresolved issues around your ego wounding and identify dysfunctional coping skills that helped you survive the wounding.

◆ The process of **reclaiming your life** includes:

♥ **learning to love yourself**

♥ **learning to protect yourself**

♥ **learning to own your reality**

♥ **learning to nurture yourself**

♥ **learning to live in moderation**

♦ When this healing/transformation occurs, your ego is awakened to its rightful role and carries out its function as the agent/artist of your soul, allowing you to experience **a conscious journey of awakening.**

♦ **You can and do live in context.** You are both **interrelated** and **interdependent** (connected with every other being and mutually dependent upon one another). Everything and everyone is **linked** as part of the same creation. All is sacred. Thus you will recognize that you are **responsible** (have the ability to respond), and that what you do or don't do affects other people. You have **a unique and important role** in the whole scheme of things. Each person has a different path. Unfortunately, you may have succumbed to the cultural pressure of 'sameness', or trying to be what you think others want.

♦ In opening to your recovery process, your unique path will unfold before you. It does not mean you are harmful, inconsiderate, or do not meet your responsibilities. It means you are moving toward **greater wholeness.** In aligning your ego with your soul, you will come to recognize that **you are both human and divine.**

♦ Your responsibility is **to participate fully in life.** Paradoxically, you will feel most separated when you are trying to control the process by holding onto something or someone. By looking deep inside yourself, you can discover your soul mission (life calling) and then trust it and trust yourself.

II. what is your soul?

♦ Like the wind that cannot be seen or contained but can be felt, **your soul** can be known by the effects of its presence and its workings in your life.

♦ The qualities that point to **your soul's reality** are infinite. Here is a partial list:

Aliveness	Autonomy	Awe	Beauty	Certainty
Clarity	Compassion	Contentment	Conviction	Courage
Devotion	Discernment	Equanimity	Faith	Freedom
Fullness	Generosity	Goodness	Grace	Gratitude
Innocence	Intelligence	Joy	Love	Loyalty
Openness	Peace	Power	Presence	Serenity
Spaciousness	Stillness	Strength	Tenderness	Truth
Unity	Value	Vitality	Wholeness	Wisdom

♦ Your soul expresses itself through qualities that are familiar to you.

♦ By bringing certain qualities to mind you can sense what your soul is like.

♦ Everyone is capable of experiencing and expressing these qualities.

♦ In each person certain qualities will be more apparent than others, and there is generally some that are more prominent than others.

♦ Learning to recognize the qualities unique to your own soul can help you identify them in others.

III. core concepts of this recovery model

♦ This model defines codependence as **a lack of connection** with your soul (a spiritual 'dis-ease'). This disconnection results in being at war with yourself (and with others).

♦ Your recovery is **the journey home** to the deepest aspect of yourself (your soul). It offers an opportunity to have a love affair with your human self along with enjoying a conscious living experience.

♦ Your recovery is **unsustainable** without transformation, and your transformation **begins** with your recovery.

♦ Your process of transformation involves **reorientation** from ego dominance (identifying primarily with your personality) to soul fulfillment (trusting and surrendering to your destiny).

♦ The following are evolving concepts of this recovery model. You are invited to keep an open mind and entertain each one from a '**What if it is true?**' perspective.

☐ You are important and valuable.

☐ You have unique gifts to express, share, and experience.

☐ You are interconnected and interdependent with all people and all life forms.

☐ Your life has meaning and purpose (regardless of your awareness).

☐ There are no 'mistakes' in your life, only loving lessons to be learned.

☐ Codependence is a learned pattern of behaviors, beliefs, and feelings.

☐ Your dysfunctional patterns cause unnecessary suffering.

☐ You can recover from your wounding by reconnecting with your spirituality.

☐ You are a spiritual being having a human experience.

☐ You are both human and divine.

☐ You are a unique manifestation of Source energy (or whatever name you prefer).

☐ You can choose the kind of relationship you have with Source energy.

☐ You can access Source energy directly without an intermediary.

☐ You are both one with Source energy and at the same time seemingly separate.

☐ Source energy is evolving through you via your life experiences.

☐ Your birthright is to live on Planet Earth in a physical body with issues to work through.

☐ When you overly identify with your human self and the affairs of the world, you live in a fear-based reality.

☐ You are here to deepen your capacity both to give and to receive love.

☐ When you are true and loving with yourself, you are true and loving with the Universe.

☐ You are here to experience your soul, and thus Planet Earth is a school of conscious awareness.

☐ Healing is about learning and integrating your life lessons.

☐ You are a system of human energy, and you can learn to regulate your energy.

☐ You and other people serve as catalysts for one another's growth and awakening.

☐ You are the co-creator of your reality.

☐ Consciously or unconsciously, you are continuing to evolve.

☐ Your human circumstances are of your creation, and they can potentially serve you.

☐ Your soul is greater than your conditions (addictions, issues, problems, emotions) and your wounding.

☐ In your core reality you are not deficient, defective, or a human failure.

☐ In your core reality you are equal to every human being: not superior to or inferior to any other. All creation is One.

☐ Your soul does not die, but continues to evolve.

☐ Your birthright is to experience soul actualization (leading to soul fulfillment).

IV. what is codependence?

♦ Codependence is not a 'disease', it's not inevitable, and it doesn't have to be a life-long affliction that will 'infect' your children. Codependence is simply a set of **maladaptive thought processes and coping patterns** that were acquired in the course of growing up.

♦ From a core sense of **internal emptiness** you feel there's something missing, and you think you will find it in relationships with others. Your family and society have conditioned you to look for **True Love** to heal your incomplete process of individuation / differentiation and fill your empty core, but you replicate your codependent patterns in every relationship you attempt. The inevitable **conflict and anguish** of your codependent relationships may lead you to dependence on substance and/or process addictions for **symptom relief**.

♦ Codependence is best understood as **a lack of attunement to who you are** in your deepest core, having no awareness of or connection with your soul, and not embracing both your humanity and your divinity.

V. origins of codependence

You learned your particular codependence patterns from a variety of life experiences and **conditioning**. Here are some major influences:

♦ **Childrearing**

To provide you with adequate nurturing, your caregivers needed to understand and accept the **nuances** of their own personal issues, including:

☐ their substance and process addictions

☐ their various mental disorders

☐ their inability to love themselves

☐ their inability to deal with stressors

☐ their beliefs about childrearing

☐ their unresolved childhood issues

☐ their arrested development

☐ their cognitive distortions

☐ their fear- and shame-based realities

☐ their black-and-white thinking

In trying to make sense of your childhood experiences, you realize that your parents **may or may not have been aware** of and worked through these conditions.

♦ **Dysfunctional Parenting Styles**

Trying to cope with their children as best they could, your parents may have resorted to these **learned** parenting styles:

☐ being critical and attacking

☐ ignoring, neglecting, or abandoning

☐ inviting the child to fail

☐ enmeshing with the child, blaming the child for the parent's feelings

♦ **Childhood Trauma**

Childhood trauma causes adults to act out their **shame issues.** Codependent caregivers repeat **controlling patterns of violence** along a continuum of **extremes:**

♥ **Physical abuse:** use of implements, face slapping, shaking, hair pulling, head banging, tickling a child into hysteria, lack of appropriate physical nurturing, and intrusive procedures (enemas).

♥ **Sexual abuse:**

☐ *physical sexual* involves intercourse, oral sex, anal sex, masturbation of the child, having a child masturbate an adult, sexual hugging.

☐ *overt/explicit* involves voyeurism or exhibitionism.

☐ *covert* involves verbal sexual abuse or lack of appropriate boundary setting with the child.

☐ *emotional sexual* involves emotional enmeshment by the parent, or the child as a witness to sexual abuse.

Studies in the addiction field have found that 80 percent of males and 75 percent of females with **substance addictions** have been **sexually abused.**

♥ **Intellectual abuse:** attacks to the child's thinking process, over-control of the expression of the child's thoughts, and failure on the part of the major caregiver to teach logical thinking and problem solving. Children are often taught *what* to think as opposed to *how* to think.

♥ **Emotional abuse:** a caregiver refuses to let a child express feelings, shames a child for his/her feelings, or demonstrates improper expression of his/her feelings in front of a child.

♥ **Spiritual abuse:**

☐ Major caregivers are disrespectful of child's reality and demand to be the child's higher Power.

☐ Perfection is demanded of the child, and the child is over-controlled.

☐ The child is ignored, neglected, or abandoned.

☐ The child is indulged.

☐ The caregivers have religious addictions.

☐ There is abuse at the hands of a religious caregiver.

☐ The caregiver does not follow stated family rules or values and/or shifts rules to suit his/her needs.

☐ There are hidden rules in the family.

◆ **Dominator Social System**

♥ Human beings have recently created a **dominator social system** in which **male dominance, violence**, and a general **hierarchic and authoritarian social structure** is now the norm.

♥ To varying degrees this model of social organization has been **ingrained in you** from the moment you were born.

♥ When you identify with your human ego, you believe that **you are separate from other human beings** and from Source energy. **This false belief** in your separation **makes all forms of violence possible.**

♥ Our current culture believes that the personality attributes of **being better than, invulnerable, perfectionistic, anti-dependent, and controlling** are healthy and something to be valued, when, in fact, they are codependent characteristics!

◆ **Codependence in relationships**

♥ You learn self-perpetuating, maladaptive patterns in **codependent relationships** with others and yourself.

♥ Codependent patterns are a **byproduct of your socialization** (your conditioning).

♥ You developed these patterns as **coping strategies** to protect yourself and meet your needs the best way you could at the time.

♥ You thought, felt, and performed these things **to survive** emotionally, mentally, and/or physically.

♥ Now these same strategies are **destructive** and keep you in **survival mode** (in fear) as opposed to becoming self-empowered.

♥ Most of these maladaptive coping strategies have become so **pervasive** that they are now **unconscious** (automatic).

VI. common experiences of codependence

- ☐ Feelings of **low self-esteem** often cause you to judge yourself and others without mercy. You compensate by trying to be perfect, taking responsibility for others, attempting to control the outcome of unpredictable events, getting angry when things don't go your way, and/or gossiping instead of confronting an issue.

- ☐ You also tend to **isolate** and feel uneasy around others, especially authority figures. You become an approval seeker and go to great lengths to have people like you.

- ☐ You are **extremely loyal**, even in the face of evidence that suggests that loyalty is undeserved.

- ☐ You are **intimidated** by angry people and personal criticism, which causes you to feel anxious and overly sensitive.

- ☐ You tend to get involved with **emotionally unavailable** people with addictive personalities, and are less attracted to healthy, caring people.

- ☐ You live life as a **victim** and are attracted to other victims in your friendship and love relationships. You confuse love with pity and tend to 'love' people you can pity and rescue.

- ☐ You tend to be **overly responsible** or **very irresponsible**. This pattern can manifest as trying to solve others' problems or expecting others to be responsible for you, both of which enable you to avoid looking closely at your own behavior.

- ☐ You often feel **guilty** when you stand up for yourself. Consequently you give in to others instead of taking care of yourself.

- ☐ You deny, minimize, or repress your **feelings** from your traumatic childhood.

- ☐ You experience difficulty **accessing/expressing** your feelings, and are unaware of the impact this has on your life.

- ☐ You are terrified of **rejection** or **abandonment**. Consequently you tend to stay in jobs or relationships that are harmful to you. Your fears either stop you from ending hurtful relationships or prevent you from entering healthy, rewarding ones.

VII. core life skills vs. patterns of codependence

There are **five core life skills** that people who are codependent find **difficult** to develop. Instead of fostering these core life skills, society supports and perpetuates five **dysfunctional patterns of codependence**:

1 Esteeming yourself from within

♥ When you are unable to experience yourself as being **valuable** (precious), you feel **either less than or better than others** (either low to non-existent self-esteem or arrogance/grandiosity). Both extremes stem from the **shaming** process in childhood.

♥ When you have low or non-existent self esteem, you try to seek out 'other esteem' in the form of your material possessions, accomplishments, educational degrees, physical appearance, impression management, who you know, etc.

2 Establishing and maintaining functional boundaries

♥ When you are unable to establish and maintain functional boundaries, you tend to make yourself **either too vulnerable or invulnerable**. You may have acquired impaired boundaries from caregivers who modeled impaired boundaries. Impaired boundaries manifest in four distinct forms:

☐ **nonexistent boundaries** that offer no protection.
☐ **damaged boundaries** that offer partial protection.
☐ **a wall** that offers total protection.
☐ **from a wall to nonexistent boundaries** and back again.

3 Owning your reality

♥ Owning your reality is about **experiencing who you are** and sharing that with other people, including your thinking, feeling, physical, and behavioral reality. Owning your reality is difficult when these aspects **are ignored, attacked, denied, or disputed**.

♥ This codependent pattern manifests in two ways: **either you don't know** what your reality is, **or you do know** what your reality is but **you don't or won't share** with anyone.

♥ When you are unable to accept **being imperfect**, it results in feeling **bad or rebellious** or **trying/pretending to be good or perfect**.

4 Identifying and meeting your needs

♥ Having difficulty identifying and meeting your needs stems from (a) **being attacked** for needing, or (b) from having your needs/wants **ignored or denied**, or (c) from having your needs and wants completely **taken care of** without someone teaching you how to take care of them yourself (including food, clothing, shelter, medical/dental care, physical and emotional nurturing, and getting time, attention, and direction from caregivers).

♥ This codependent pattern ranges from **being too dependent to being anti-dependent** (or needless/wantless). This pattern manifests in four ways:

☐ You are **too dependent**. You know your wants and needs, but expect others to take care of them for you.

☐ You are **anti-dependent**. You know your needs but insist on meeting them yourself and are unable to accept help or guidance.

☐ You are **needless/wantless** and don't even know that you have needs or wants.

☐ You **confuse** your wants and your needs. You know and get what you want, but don't know what you need. You try to take care of your needs by trying to get everything you want.

5 Living in moderation

♥ **Having little or no ability to be moderate** manifests as an extreme **either/or** syndrome. This codependent pattern is expressed as **living your reality in extremes**: either **no expression** of your physicality, thinking, feeling, and behavior or **crisis-like eruptions**. It's a movement from being spontaneous and open to being **out of control** or **controlling** of others. This pattern comes from experiencing only immoderate behavior from caregivers.

VIII. embracing change in your recovery

Chaos is an inherent component of a transformational process.
You can't have one without the other.
Chaos is an indication that change is in the midst of occurring.
Instead of shrinking from chaos/change, embrace it fully as an opportunity for growth!

The five core patterns of codependence are **pervasive, mutually reinforcing, and resistant** to change. This recovery program will assist you to **break through** your resistance, **experience** your authentic self, and **reclaim** your life. You will learn to:

☐ **modify** your limiting beliefs, thought forms, perceptions, attitudes, and behaviors.

☐ **develop** your motivation, patience, stamina, determination, endurance, and courage.

☐ **ask** for help and guidance from trustworthy people.

☐ **move** out of 'victim' consciousness.

☐ **honor** your uniqueness.

☐ **activate** your personal will.

☐ **take** individual responsibility.

☐ **hold yourself** accountable.

☐ **trust** and surrender.

☐ **develop** faith in a higher Power.

☐ **accept** grace (that you are unconditionally loved by a higher Power).

IX. benefits of healing the wounds of codependence

Psychospiritual healing and recovery from codependence is **a transformative learning process** that facilitates these experiences:

1 As you learn to **esteem yourself from within:**

- ☐ you become your own **best friend and ally**.
- ☐ you come to **your own rescue**.
- ☐ you begin to **like as well as love yourself**.
- ☐ you start to **respect and honor yourself**.
- ☐ you claim **your birthright** to be in a physical body.
- ☐ you develop a **deep trust** in yourself.

2 As you learn to **establish and maintain functional boundaries:**

- ☐ you feel more **confident, safe, and assured** with yourself and others.
- ☐ you learn to **direct and redirect** your mind.
- ☐ your actions become **congruent** with your words and thoughts.
- ☐ you become **assertive**.
- ☐ you dare to take **personal risks** and make your own decisions.
- ☐ you experience **intimacy** in your life.

3 As you learn to **own all aspects of your reality:**

- ☐ you come to **embrace your humanity**.
- ☐ you become **emotionally present** with yourself and others.
- ☐ you begin to **live in the here-and-now**.
- ☐ you become **more aware**.
- ☐ you accept the reality of your **body's experience**.
- ☐ you begin to **speak your truth**.

4 As you learn to **identify and meet your needs:**

- ☐ you develop effective **communication skills**.
- ☐ you become **empowered** on all levels (intellectual, emotional, physical, spiritual).
- ☐ you learn to **nurture yourself**.
- ☐ you start living up to **your full potential**.
- ☐ you become **interdependent** with all of creation.
- ☐ you experience **gratitude**.

5 As you learn to **live in moderation:**

☐ you experience a **balanced life**.

☐ you learn to **respond to life** instead of reacting.

☐ you will not need to be **the center of attention**.

☐ you can **move out of the drama** of your story.

☐ you experience becoming **calm and peaceful**.

6 As you learn to **tune into your soul's wisdom:**

☐ you begin to **align** your personality with your soul.

☐ you track your experiences and integrate your **insights, gifts, and lessons**.

☐ you develop and balance your **masculine and feminine** aspects.

☐ you become **authentic** (individuated/differentiated).

☐ you understand that you are **both human and divine**.

☐ you discover **your calling** in life (your vocation).

☐ you move out of fear and into **love**.

☐ you develop **mindfulness**.

☐ you access your **longing**.

☐ you become open to **possibilities**.

☐ you live in **hope**.

personal notes:

2. healthy self-esteem

I find it difficult to take these western psychiatrists at all seriously. Yet perhaps one ought to, for half-knowledge is a powerful thing and can be a great obstacle to the truth. They look from down up and explain the higher lights from the lower obscurities, but the foundation of these things is above and not below. The significance of the lotus is not to be found by analyzing the secrets of the mud from which it grows. Its secret is found in the heavenly archetype of the lotus that blooms forever in the light above.

—Sri Aurobindo

Remember that we are spiritual beings in human form, and that all we have to do is evoke that and we will bring spirit back into our lives. —Darcy S. Clarke

I. learning self-esteem

♦ Individuals who know that they have **inherent worth that is equal to others** have healthy self-esteem. It cannot be altered by their failings or strengths (their humanity). When negative events occur, a person with healthy self-esteem does not question his/her own worth or value! It is in this esteeming that you come to know that '**I was born precious. I am enough. I am adequate.**'

♦ When you have low self-esteem, you tend to believe that you are **less than** or **better than** others and have a maladaptive coping style.

♦ People with low self-esteem rely on the **opinions** of others to determine their worth, or they achieve a sense of self-worth by **comparing** themselves to others, expending enormous amount of energy on impression management!

♦ Regardless of the type of esteem that codependents display, it is not self-esteem. It is '**other esteem**', based on **external** things: how they look, who they know, how large their salary is, what kind of car they drive, how well their children perform, how powerful, important, or attractive their spouse is, how well they perform activities in which others value excellence, or the prestige of their earned degrees.

♦ A codependent person becomes a '**human doing**' rather than a human being. His/her self-esteem is not self-based/self-generated, but instead is created by **caretaking and people-pleasing**.

♦ The difficulty with 'other esteem' is that its source is **outside** of the person and thus **vulnerable** to changes beyond the codependent's control. Because of this, 'other esteem' is **fragile and undependable**.

♦ People with low self-esteem **fluctuate** between feeling disempowered (less than others) and falsely empowered (better than others).

♦ Finding the **middle ground** is the key, a process involving learning to esteem yourself from within.

II. origin in family systems

♦ One of the five characteristics inherent in your humanness is that **you are valuable**. It is the responsibility of caregivers (including all authority figures, especially the primary caregivers) to assist children to develop the understanding that they are valuable. If this occurs, by the time the child enters into adulthood, he/she will become a mature, functional adult who feels good about him/herself.

♦ Children absorb the esteem parents have for them. This **internalized esteem** from parents becomes the basis of self-esteem. Healthy children can esteem themselves as their parents/caregivers esteem them. Low or nonexistent self-esteem is due to caregivers' **insufficient nurturing** around their inherent worth as human beings.

♦ Parents who are able to affirm, nurture, and set limits with their children without disempowering or falsely empowering them create children who can functionally esteem themselves from within. Their self-esteem is based on **their very existence**, not on their 'human doing.'

♦ In some dysfunctional family systems children are taught to see others' mistakes and to **find fault** with others. People raised in these families tend to believe that they are superior to others (one-up or better-than), which comes across in their arrogance and grandiosity.

♦ In some dysfunctional family systems children may experience being excessively **shamed** by their caregivers, but learn that feeling superior to others helps them to feel better about themselves.

♦ In some dysfunctional family systems children are taught that they are **superior** to other people, giving them a false sense of power. In these families the children are treated as if they can do no wrong.

III. strategies for building self-esteem

☐ Free yourself from '**shoulds**'. Live your life based on what is **possible** for you along with what **feels right** instead of what you or others think you should do. 'Shoulds' get in your way from identifying and fulfilling your own needs, abilities, interests, and personal goals. Channel your energy into discovering what you want and what you are good at. Value these and take actions designed to fulfill your potential.

☐ Avoid **perfectionism**. Perfectionism paralyzes you and keeps you from accomplishing your goals.

☐ Get in touch with your own **creative energy**. Getting regular exercise will energize your body. Dance, poetry, listening to music, communing with nature, meditating, yoga, tai chi, etc. can all be useful creative outlets.

☐ **Respect** yourself.

☐ **Celebrate** your life.

☐ Act in accordance with your own **values** (principles, standards, or qualities you consider worthwhile or desirable).

☐ Identify and meet your **needs** (differentiate between your human and soul needs).

☐ Don't take things so **personally**. When someone is being rude, it is about them, their pain or fear. What they are thinking and feeling in the moment is their reality, **not yours**.

☐ Don't take life so **seriously**. Learn to see both the serious and the humorous side to every situation (learn to laugh with yourself for your humanness). Remember that all the circumstances that befall you (regardless of how difficult or painful) are serving the needs of your soul. This does not mean that you have to like your experiences or understand them.

☐ Meet **new challenges**. View challenges as opportunities for growth. As you meet new challenges, you gain new confidence and enhance your sense of accomplishment.

☐ Set **achievable goals** based on what you can realistically achieve. Work step-by-step to achieve your goals.

☐ Talk to yourself positively. Do **affirmations**.

☐ Establish and maintain healthy, functional **boundaries**.

☐ **Challenge** any negative self-talk and **counteract** it with self-affirming statements.

☐ Experience success. Look for projects that **stretch** but do not overwhelm you. Experience good feelings about your success.

☐ Take **risks**. Expect to make mistakes, but feel good about trying something new.

☐ Solve problems. Face them—**don't avoid them**. Identify ways to solve them. Take action. If you run away from problems that you can solve, you threaten your self-confidence.

☐ Make decisions. Determine **what is right for you** and deal with the consequences.

☐ **Develop** your skills. Know what you can and cannot do.

☐ Emphasize your **strengths** and focus on what you can do.

☐ Rely on your own **opinion of yourself**. Entertain feedback from others, but don't rely on their opinions for your self-esteem.

☐ Be **honest**—with yourself and everyone else.

☐ Own **your reality**—the circumstances you experience, what you sense in your body, and how you think, feel, and intuit.

IV. techniques to aid change

You are your own best therapist, and becoming your own **best friend/ally** is key. **Learning to love yourself** from within is how to heal from low self-esteem.

☐ Utilize **experiential** techniques to facilitate right brain functioning: getting out of your head and into feelings.

☐ Stay in the present moment; practice **mindfulness**.

☐ **Self-dialoging** done aloud, or with your inner child.

☐ **Visualization** to relax, draw forth, and release.

☐ **Breathwork** to bring awareness into your body, center, access feelings, and release.

☐ **Music** (both with and without words) to access feelings, memories, etc.

☐ **Movement** to release energy, to get into your body, and to express.

☐ **Journal writing** to track yourself and to document insight.

☐ **Catharsis** to release blocked feelings—yelling into a pillow, etc.

☐ **Affirmations** to claim your truth, dispel the toxins.

☐ **Artwork** (all media) used to activate imagination.

☐ **Ceremony** to center, set intentions, call forth guidance.

☐ **Vision questing** to seek revelations.

☐ Cleansing **diet** to purify and strengthen your body.

☐ Reflection/Contemplation/**Meditation**.

☐ **Sound** (self-produced).

☐ Commune with **nature**.

☐ Cognitive/Behavioral **restructuring**: positive affirmations, reframing, changing habits.

☐ **Dreamwork** (self-interpretation).

☐ Use **body sensations and symptoms** to access information at the deepest level.

☐ **Forgiveness** of yourself and others.

☐ Effective **communication** skills (asking for wants and needs).

☐ **Boundary-setting**.

☐ **Shadow work** to accept and integrate what has been disowned within yourself.

☐ Develop your **intuition**.

☐ Become your own **best friend/ally**.

☐ Practice **yoga**/tai chi, etc.

☐ **Read** spiritual and self-help texts (to inspire and educate).

☐ Build your **support network**: surround yourself with an inner and outer circle of friends who are on a similar path.

V.   affirmations: you are what you think and affirm

♦ There is a great deal of **power** in thoughts, in spoken words, and in written statements that you make about yourself.

♦ There is a **direct connection** between the way you think about yourself and how you behave. It is difficult and **awesome** for you to imagine how much of your own reality you create by how you think and speak. You do **create your own realities** with your thoughts, however, and your thoughts and attitudes contribute to the healing process.

♦ In order to increase your self-esteem, you need to begin thinking **positive, loving thoughts** about yourself. And you can begin to do this through affirmations.

♦ Affirmations are positive thoughts that you **deliberately** introduce into your consciousness so that the old, negative programming is replaced by new and positive thoughts. It is vital to remember that affirmations are not used to **repress** feelings. Nor are they used to **stuff** emotions. Chemically dependent and codependent people have a great deal of experience with **how** to stuff feelings and emotions. Affirmations create **a new and fresh point of view**, and they help to **raise** your self-esteem, whereas before treatment you had none at all.

♦ The following guidelines are helpful when learning how to use affirmations:

1. Affirmations are **positive** statements. The point of an affirmation is to affirm the positive rather than reinforce the negative.

2. Affirmations are most effective when they are **short** and to the point.

3. Keep your affirmations in the **present**.

4. Remember that affirmations are used to affirm what you **desire** rather than what you might want to get rid of.

5. Affirmations **take time** to get results. They should not be put on a timetable. The results will unfold at their own speed—not at yours or mine. Be **patient**.

6. Affirmations need to be **repeated** each day. It is the repetition of the positive affirmation that produces the desired result.

♦ The most powerful way to use affirmations is to **write** them down on paper. As you write your affirmation, you see it, you say it, and you begin to feel it.

♦ Following are some affirmations that might work for you. Start with a few of these and **believe in yourself**. Repeat your affirmation several times in succession. As you go through the day, pause and go back to your affirmation and repeat it another three times. Do this throughout the day, each day, until the affirmation becomes **a part of you** and you believe in yourself.

♥ I am a child of God.

♥ I am a precious person.

♥ I am a worthwhile person.

♥ I am beautiful inside and outside.

♥ I love myself unconditionally.

♥ I deserve to be loved by myself and others.

♥ I am loved because I deserve love.

♥ I forgive myself for letting others hurt me.

♥ I am a child of God, and I deserve love, peace, prosperity, and serenity.

♥ I am willing to accept love.

♥ I am not alone; I am one with God and the universe.

♥ I am capable of changing.

♥ I am enough.

VI. experiential activities

1. On respecting yourself: What do you respect about yourself? If you get stuck, think of people who admire you or have admired you—what would they say about you? (This exercise is good as a 'check-in'.)

2. On values: What are your values? Write them down and discuss them with others.

3. On needs: Identify the needs of your soul (love, greater connection with self, others, higher Power, living, self-actualization, increased consciousness/awareness, serenity, peace, contentment, fulfillment, meaning/purpose). Allow yourself to have your loftiest dreams and needs. Write them down and share them with someone you trust.

3. transforming shame

One moment we feel fine, then we notice a stain on our shirt or the boss is criticizing us for a mistake. We would like to stay cool and composed, if only our bodies would cooperate! We are getting warm, our face is turning red, we cannot force our eyes to look forward, our chest becomes heavy, our heart might pound, we have an empty sensation in our gut. Time crawls by as we struggle in the grip of acute self-consciousness. We can barely talk, we are ashamed, we fight a compelling urge to retreat, to run. We feel nauseated. We might have brief hesitations in our speech, glance away while talking, delicately shift our conversation. We may have barely noticeable feelings of facial warmth and discomfort, feel smaller and smaller while persons around us seem to get bigger, louder and more dangerous. It seems like we're shrinking, pulled inward, instinctively taking up less room. We are trying to protect ourselves and feel like a very young child. We feel open, vulnerable and exposed. Our skin seems to become transparent so that others see right through us ... We are having a 'shame attack'.

I.   what is shame?

- Shame-based reality is **a spiritual crisis** that develops as a result of emotional and/or physical abandonment.

- **Physical abandonment** is blatant: inadequate nurturing around basic needs (food, clothing, shelter, medical/dental needs) or healthy physical attention.

- **Emotional abandonment** is more covert: a failure to provide adequate emotional nurturing due to unavailability, put-downs, and parental indifference to meeting your needs and wants, including education, spiritual nurturance, sexuality information, etc.

- When you hide, invalidate, minimize, judge/blame, or deny your feelings, **you abandon yourself.**

- **Shame-based reality** leads you to believe that you should not exist, that you are 'something wrong'. You believe that **you are a mistake**, that even God despises you, and that you are unworthy of love. As a result you lose your sense of communion with others and connection with your soul and your higher Power, so that you become isolated from all external sources of comfort. You feel tremendous loneliness at the center of your being and don't know who you are or why you are here. You experience life as having no meaning or purpose. As the emptiness and feelings of worthlessness grow, you may even consider suicide.

II.   feelings of guilt

- Guilt is about actions: **doing something you know is wrong** (a failure of *doing*: stealing, lying, cheating, etc.). When you have done something against your values, **you fear punishment**. The degree of guilt you feel is equal to the transgression.

- Guilt is a healthy and necessary sense that you have **violated** a moral code (your own values/standards), or that you have **intruded** on someone else's rights. You broke clear, specific rules.

- Guilt leads to **accountability** and respect for others' rights and personal growth.

23

III. common responses to a shame attack

☐ The **bond** between you and the other person is broken.

☐ You feel **exposed** and because of this, you fear abandonment.

☐ The **chasm** widens between you and the other person because you go away to hide.

☐ There is a tendency to **abuse yourself** emotionally, intellectually, physically, or a combination of the above.

☐ The person who shamed you (or who you *think* shamed you) tries to approach you, and you feel even more exposed.

☐ You fight, freeze, flee, throw up defenses, become enraged, become controlling, become perfectionistic, and/or numb out.

☐ You retreat out of a desire for self-preservation; the chasm widens further, and as a result, you feel abandoned, hearing 'I was right: I am no good' and similar messages.

☐ This creates more shame, leading to more isolation and more abandonment *ad nauseum*.

IV. healthy shame vs. toxic shame

♦ **Healthy shame** is a **necessary** feeling and can manifest when you have made a mistake and are being seen; you feel embarrassed and exposed. It makes you aware that you are fallible; this leads you to hold yourself accountable for your behaviors.

♦ The **gifts** of healthy shame are **humility** (making mistakes), **containment** (living in connection with others), and **humanity** (being imperfect).

♦ Healthy shame allows you to **see your imperfections** and still like yourself.

♦ Healthy shame lets you know that **you can go too far**—that you need to pull back and be responsible for your negative impact on others (leading to accountability).

♦ Healthy shame makes you aware of **the need for a higher Power** for guidance, solace, serenity.

♦ Healthy shame is **helpful** in moderation, but **damaging** when you are unable to release it.

♦ **Toxic shame** is shame-based reality where you believe that something is basically wrong with you: that you are a mistake, that you are too flawed to be wanted or valued, fearing abandonment and bothered by your shortcomings. You have the painful belief in your basic **defectiveness** as a human being.

♦ Toxic shame is **more difficult to heal than guilt** because it is about you as a person as opposed to your actions. The shame-based person has taken his/her shame into the very center of his/her being.

♦ Toxic shame is about your **self worth** and is about a **failure** of your *being*. Thus **you fear abandonment**.

♦ You can experience **both shame and guilt** at the same time. For example, the spouse who has broken his/her vow to be faithful may be full of remorse and might say 'I have done something very bad' (guilt) but might also believe that 'I am a weak, defective, or disgusting person, and there is something inherently wrong with me' (toxic shame).

♦ Toxic shame is **a feeling with a set of physical responses** combined with predictable actions, uncomfortable thoughts, and spiritual pain and despair (looking down/blushing, hiding/withdrawing from others, believing that 'I'm a failure in life' or that 'I have no purpose here'). When you feel shamed, you feel too flawed to be wanted or valued by others, and you expect the other person to leave you as soon as he/she realizes that you are less than perfect.

♦ In **shame-based reality** you are usually bothered by **your shortcomings**, while **your guilt** simply shows you **your transgressions** that can be changed. When you operate from shame-based reality you see yourself as failing to reach your goals in life, not as smart as your fellow workers, not as attractive, not as kind, not as interesting, and not good enough, etc. Whereas when you simply feel guilt, you say to yourself, 'I wish I hadn't done that. I have harmed others and feel regret.'

♦ Sometimes the problems of shame and guilt **blend** into each other until it is almost **impossible to distinguish** between these. When you begin with the question, 'How could I have done something like that?', you may be focusing attention on either the 'that' or the 'I' part of the question. 'How could I have done *that?*' implies concern about behavior, transgression, and guilt. 'How could *I* have done that?' concerns personal identity, shortcomings, and shame.

V.   signs that shame exists

☐ Rage/extreme amounts of anger.

☐ Power struggles about who is right or wrong.

☐ 'All or nothing' thinking.

☐ Blaming others for your problems.

☐ Continually striving for perfection.

☐ Striving for power and control over others.

☐ Being overly competitive.

☐ Physical abuse of others.

☐ Withdrawal, leading to loneliness and isolation.

☐ Low self-esteem.

☐ Feeling guilt-ridden much of the time.

☐ Being preoccupied with your 'image' (how you appear to others).

☐ Grandiosity / self-righteousness / contempt for others / taking a 'one-up' position.

☐ Depression.

☐ Substance and/or process addictions.

☐ Defensiveness (minimizing, denying, intellectualizing).

☐ Rapid deflation of the self.

☐ Sudden loss of energy.

VI. sources of shame

No single source of shame applies to everyone. Here are several:

♦ **The dominator model** of social organization and societal values (cultural bias, discrimination, technocratic, materialistic, and egocentric). Society often shames you.

♦ **Families of origin:** living in a family system where caregivers are critical, judgmental, and unsupportive. When a caregiver abuses a child, the caregiver is out of touch with his/her own healthy shame. If the parent were in touch with healthy shame, he/she would stop abusing the child. As a result of physical and/or emotional abuse by a shaming parent, the child develops a core of shame that the parent induced during the abuse. **(Mellody 100)**

♦ **Shame-based families:**

☐ Family members say and do things that create and perpetuate shame.

☐ One or two family members are singled out for shame as scapegoats who get blamed for everything and are given the whole family's shame. **(Potter-Efron 74)**

☐ Scapegoats often believe that they will always be branded as bad, dumb, or worthless and will carry their shame into adulthood, expecting always to be judged.

☐ In these families the daily routine is full of insults and personality attacks.

☐ Shame-based families cannot or do not control shaming behavior; members often seem to attack each other.

☐ As an adult you must take responsibility for your own shame.

☐ It is important to learn how parents, siblings, grandparents, teachers, etc., contributed to your shame in order to begin alleviating it.

♦ **Deficiency messages:**

☐ Children who **feel defective** have often been told over and over that something is wrong with them. Eventually they **internalize** these messages and then repeat them to themselves: 'You are not good.' 'You are not good enough.' 'You do not belong.' 'You are not lovable.' 'You should not exist.' **(Ibid. 76)**

☐ 'You have always been ... fat, ugly, stupid, crazy, etc. ... that's just the way you are, you can't change ... from the moment you were born, I could tell that something was wrong...' When a parent *actually believes* this statement, a child can do nothing to make the parent think or act otherwise. The child becomes **spiritually wounded**, seeing no reason for his/her existence.

☐ No matter what these children do, they cannot gain parental approval. Their parents always seem disappointed in them, but are quick to point out that they have great potential. These children believe that they will **never be able to do enough**. They keep trying to the point of exhaustion and carry this desperation into adulthood, marrying mates who repeat the same pattern of non-acceptance and disappointment. **(Ibid. 77)**

☐ These children often **feel different** from the rest of the family: something about them is **unacceptable** (red hair, too smart, mother/father failed to bond with them).

Whatever the reason, the rest of the family seems closer to each other. The child may be very sensitive to nonverbal rejection (a small shrug of disinterest, a concealed yawn, rolled eyes). (Ibid.)

☐ A child depends entirely on being lovable. They need that as a guarantee that they will be protected, sheltered, and fed. Yet no child can earn another's love; no child can make his parents love him. Therefore he concludes that **something must be wrong** with him. (After all, other children are loved by their parents.) Unloved children are not necessarily physically abused or neglected. They might simply be **tolerated** in their families. They are seldom, if ever, *told* that they are loved. A parent might turn away or suddenly refuse to speak to the child. Threats are terrifying to the child. Parents who threaten to withdraw their love use **the fear of abandonment** to control their children, damaging the child's sense of worth in the process. When the parents imply that the child is worth loving only when he/she behaves, this message contributes to excessive shame. (Ibid. 78)

◆ **Current shaming relationships:** do you have to hide a part of yourself to be accepted or be perfect?

◆ Your own **self-shaming thoughts, words, and behaviors:** doing onto yourself what was done unto you is not caring for yourself. You focus on failures and shortcomings and constantly call yourself shaming names.

◆ **Inherited shame:** family secrets carry and/or hide unresolved trauma that was experienced in the family before you were born.

◆ **Self-hatred** develops when you add to your shame by **replaying** your embarrassments, defeats, and humiliations and calling yourself **derogatory and shaming names**.

VII. shaming thoughts

◆ When you have a shame-based reality, shaming thoughts usually occur with great regularity. You assume everyone thinks this way, and that others agree with your own self-evaluation. Thus you **expect ridicule** and disdain.

◆ Shame that cannot be removed gradually turns into **self-hatred** (one insult at a time!) and creates a **'black hole'** in your soul into which your goodness vanishes, leaving a residue of disgust and contempt for yourself.

◆ When you are feeling inadequate, 'less-than', stupid, ugly, insufficient, dirty, worthless, or the like, you are experiencing **toxic shame**. A message becomes a belief when you repeat it over and over again.

☐ **I am defective,** damaged, broken, a mistake, flawed.

☐ **I am dirty,** soiled, ugly, unclean, impure, filthy, disgusting.

☐ **I am incompetent,** not good enough, inept, ineffective.

☐ **I am unwanted,** unloved, unappreciated, uncherished.

☐ **I am nothing,** worthless, invisible, unnoticed, empty.

☐ **I am weak,** small, impotent, puny, feeble.

☐ **I am bad,** awful, dreadful, evil, despicable.

- [ ] **I am pitiful,** contemptible, miserable, insignificant.
- [ ] **I deserve criticism**, condemnation, disapprovals.
- [ ] **I deserve to be abandoned,** forgotten, unloved, left out.

VIII. maladaptive/painful ways of coping with shame

Your natural response to shaming experiences is to hide and withdraw, and the last thing you want to do is talk about this feeling.

- [ ] **Paralysis**: you are unable to do anything, may want to speak but no words come out, may want to run but cannot, become stuck. This may intensify your shame, and you may attack yourself for not being strong enough to stand up for yourself.

- [ ] **Faltering Energy:** shame steals energy, just as it diminishes self-worth, so that you feel smaller, weaker, less potent, or very 'young'.

- [ ] **Escapism:** you feel overwhelmed in social situations and attempt to withdraw from others and seek private, secure places where none can see your shame. You may become a very private person who prefers to spend time alone.

- [ ] **Social Masks/False Personas:** more subtle than running away, you may develop elaborate masks to cover your real self. You might smile a lot, always try to please others, and appear self-confident and comfortable. You become convinced that others would despise you if they could see past your masks to your real self. You try to keep your shame a secret, withdraw emotionally, and put on a 'good act'.

- [ ] **Perfectionism:** you reason that you will have nothing to feel ashamed about if you never make a mistake, and therefore you become a perfectionist. You do not accept your human imperfections and believe that errors advertise your shame. The more shame you have, the more you feel the need to be perfect in order to be accepted.

- [ ] **Criticism/Judgment:** you attempt to throw off your painful feelings of shame by becoming critical of everyone, making others appear flawed, ridiculous, stupid, idiotic, or uneducated. You are eager to point out the weaknesses of others. You attempt to rid yourself of your shame feelings by noticing everyone else's imperfections, thus drawing attention away from your own. You can take this to extremes and become arrogant, believing that you are better than everyone else in order to avoid experiencing your own intolerable shame.

- [ ] **Rage:** you fight back against humiliation by attacking the supposed aggressor. By attacking the personalities of others, you unconsciously defend your own fragile identity. When you combine shame with rage you may become verbally or physically abusive.

- [ ] **Controlling**: you try to control other people, your environment, and your own thoughts and feelings.

- [ ] **Victim:** in 'victim mode' you do not know how to say 'No', do not establish and maintain boundaries, do not realize that you have (or should have) needs, and develop a high tolerance for inappropriate behavior.

IX. healing your relationship to shame

- ♦ The goal is to learn how to appreciate yourself more as a valuable human being with **important gifts** to contribute to the world!

28   © 2013 Darcy S. Clarke info@LivingInAlignment.ca

◆ When something hurtful has been internalized, you need to be able to say, *'But that's **not about me**—its not about my worth or identity. Yes, it hurt! Yes, it felt horrible! Yes, it caused me problems in my life, but it's not about my core self. I'm not my shame!'* Owning the sadness, hurt, fear, anger, guilt, and shame is necessary to heal your woundedness, so that you can let go and move on.

◆ **Is it possible? Yes!** You will need energy, patience, persistence, understanding, courage, hope, and a deep faith that nobody needs to remain forever in personal despair.

◆ When you start healing your shame **you will become more accepting of your humanity, become more autonomous, feel more competent, and become more humble.** You will be able to say, 'I'm human, no better or worse than others, unique and good enough as I am!' You will truly love yourself with all of your imperfections, and as a result will learn to really love others as well.

◆ People who are healing from a shame-based reality discover they are freer to live lives that center around self-respect, dignity, honor, and realistic pride.

X. experiencing love and forgiveness

◆ Healing from your shame-based reality requires that you gain an understanding of the **cause-and-effect** relationships between the impact of less-than-nurturing childhood experiences and the effect they had on the adult you became.

◆ This understanding entails both recognizing and acknowledging events and experiences and doing emotional release work.

◆ It is imperative that you acknowledge on an emotional level that **you were powerless** to do anything any differently than you did.

◆ Making this connection with your **emotional wounding** is absolutely necessary before you can truly start to love yourself.

◆ Having **compassion** for yourself is often the most difficult step!

◆ As a child you felt **responsible** for the things that happened to you. You **blamed yourself** for the things that were done to you and for the deprivations you suffered.

◆ In order to heal, to unplug your energies from the past, you must go back to that child who still exists within you and say, '**It wasn't your fault**. You didn't do anything wrong. You were just a kid!'

◆ Being able to say '**I love you**' to the child within you, and to the person you are today, and really mean it on an emotional level, is another important goal.

◆ Until you can forgive and love yourself, you cannot truly **love and forgive** any other human beings, including your parents, who were doing the best they knew how, given their level of consciousness. They too were powerless to do anything differently; they were **reacting** to their wounds.

◆ It is absolutely necessary to **own the reality of your childhood** in order to love the person you are today! You do this by owning the experiences of your childhood, honoring the feelings associated with these experiences, and releasing the emotional **energy of grief** that you are still carrying around!

◆ Remember that **HOPE** is the antidote to despair!

XI. action steps on your journey out of shame

1. Become fully **aware of your shame. Face your shame** directly. Speak your **truth**.

2. **Be gentle** with yourself. Offer yourself understanding and compassion.

3. **Be patient** with yourself. The wounds of shaming are deep and long-lasting. Healing from shame-based reality is a gradual process that won't always go smoothly.

4. Identify your **defense** mechanisms. They hide your shame. Understand how your defenses **protect yourself** from painful shame feelings and thoughts (This is not about just getting rid of your defenses). Investigate the **sources** of your shame.

5. Identify your **addictions**. They medicate shame.

6. **Accept** a certain amount of shame as part of the **imperfect human experience**.

7. **Challenge shame** by changing your self-concept, accessing your inherent worth, and affirming your birthright to exist.

8. Challenge **assaults on your self-worth** that occur during biochemically induced depression.

9. **Stop** shaming yourself. **Set positive goals** for yourself to help replace your shame with authentic self-worth based on your humanity, humility, autonomy, and competence. Take mental and physical action to move toward those goals. Review your progress regularly.

10. Keep in the forefront that you have **a right** to feel good about yourself and your life.

11. Access and **nurture** both your human needs and your soul needs.

12. Be **honest** with yourself and others in all of your affairs. **Participate fully** in your life.

13. Begin to assume that trusted others have **good intentions** towards you.

14. Join and **participate** in recovery groups (such as attending 12-step meetings).

15. **Expose** your shame: talk about it with trusted friends, colleagues, safe family members (who do not add to your shame and humiliation). Translate your shame into **emotional pain** and express it with others in a safe and supportive environment.

16. Examine your **attachment** to your shame. Be aware of your 'secondary gains'. Identify how you are **acting out** and stop doing it.

17. **Find** a sponsor or therapist: someone who is willing to listen and support you in healing from shame.

18. Modify and/or **change** your limiting beliefs, perceptions, and attitudes.

19. Learn to move from the literal to the **symbolic** interpretation of both past and present events and circumstances.

20. Take quality time **alone** every day as a means to center yourself. Develop **mindfulness** and your 'observer self.' **Practice** affirmations daily.

21. Learn to **re-parent** yourself. Tune into your feelings and **express** them appropriately.

22. Establish and maintain healthy **boundaries**.

23. Make **conscious** your patterns of responding. Stop and observe your thoughts, feelings, and experiences without judging or blaming yourself.

24. Consciously **monitor** your interactions and patterns with others, staying alert for situations that trigger old shaming scenes that create shame for you in the present.

25. Learn to be **in charge** of how you react/respond to and behave in everyday situations.

26. **Stop** criticizing yourself. Stop striving to be perfect. **Let go** of resentment. **Release** the past by forgiving yourself and others.

27. **Accept your human reality** (what is happening in the here-and-now: difficult life circumstances that befall you, physical pain, emotional discomfort, etc.). Learn to love, respect, and approve of yourself. **Celebrate** your life. Seek out lost **dignity** and competence in yourself.

28. Stay **current** with everyone in your life. Seek out partnerships that are **growth** enhancing. **Gravitate** to people who are committed to their personal growth, to living life fully, and who have both the desire and the capacity to be in co-committed (interdependent) relationships.

29. Let go of your **controlling** behavior. **Allow** others the 'freedom to be' and to fail. Become more **spontaneous**. Trust and surrender.

30. Investigate your spiritual connections and disconnections; develop your **spirituality**.

31. Develop a sense of **hope**. Keep telling yourself that you are a **spark** of the divine, that you are inherently valuable and precious, that you are **worthy** of love, that your life has **meaning** and purpose, that you are here to make a **contribution** to the world, and that your **birthright** is to be here.

32. Learn to live in **moderation**.

XII. experiential exercises

1. Recognize without judgment when you are having a shame attack by accessing your 'observer self'. Notice your physical sensations. Breathe in loving kindness/gentleness and compassion. Notice your feelings and thoughts.

2. Exercise: counteracting shame

   a. Identify a limiting or negative belief about yourself.

   b. Repeat it slowly out loud 12 times and take in the words.

   c. Report the sensations in your body and the feelings that arise.

   d. Breathe into your body sensations and feelings.

   e. Simultaneously allow yourself to go back in time to the event where the negative belief first originated. What was the context?

   f. Identify who gave you the shaming message.

   g. See the event and person(s) in your mind's eye.

   h. Identify and be with your feelings that arise when you do this.

   i. Take the gifts of **anger** (assertiveness, strength, energy), **fear** (preservation, wisdom, protection), and **pain** (healing, growth, awareness) and channel this energy into challenging the shaming message with a self-affirming statement.

   j. This is an opportunity to become your own best ally, to come to your own rescue, to release yourself from the grip of the past.

   k. Choose someone from the group to represent the shaming message and choose someone else to counteract that message with a self-affirming statement (rotate other people into those roles during the exercise).

3. Forgiveness Process (didactic exercise).

4. 'Walkabout' Process: sit in circle, one person at a time will walk 3 times inside the circle (clockwise) while everyone else tunes into that person's essence/soul/spirit. After the walk, people give feedback about what of that person's essence they saw, heard, felt, or experienced. Walker can then give response and new walker chooses him/herself.

XIII. homework

Make a list of all of your **negative self-talk** and bring it to the next meeting. Keep the list simple and direct.

shame worksheet

how to intervene lovingly in a shame attack

A. Awareness and acceptance of your reality is the key!

1. What is the precipitating event / 'trigger'?

_____

_____

_____

_____

2. Identify and 'breathe into' your body sensations (check & circle words that apply):

☐ **Face:** blushing, warmth, tingling, tightness in jaw, other:_____

☐ **Chest:** heart pounding, tightness, heaviness, other: _____

☐ **Stomach:** nausea, butterflies, tightness, other: _____

☐ **Shoulders/neck/back:** tightness, pain, other: _____

☐ **Overall body:** warmth, weakness, shrinking, other: _____

☐ **Other:** _____

3. What are your thoughts/negative self talk? (check & circle words that apply)

☐ **I am defective**: damaged, broken, a mistake, flawed

☐ **I am dirty**: soiled, ugly, unclean, impure, filthy, disgusting

☐ **I am incompetent**: not good enough, inept, ineffective

☐ **I am unwanted**: unloved, unappreciated, uncherished

☐ **I deserve to be abandoned**: forgotten, unloved, left out

☐ **I am weak**: small, impotent, puny, feeble

☐ **I am bad**: awful, dreadful, evil, despicable

☐ **I am pitiful**: contemptible, miserable, insignificant

☐ **I am nothing**: worthless, invisible, unnoticed, empty

☐ **I deserve criticism, condemnation, disapproval.**

☐ **I should not be having these thoughts, feelings and body sensations.**

☐ **Other:** _____

4. **Noticing your 'defenses'/coping mechanisms ('fight', 'flee', or 'freeze'), check the items that apply to you:**

☐ **Paralysis:** unable to do anything, may want to speak but no words come out, may want to run but cannot, then may attack yourself for being weak.

☐ **Faltering Energy:** shame steals energy just as it diminishes self-worth, so that you feel smaller, weaker, less potent, or very 'young'.

☐ **Escapism:** you feel overwhelmed in social situations and attempt to withdraw from others, seeking private, secure places where no one can see your shame.

☐ **Social Masks/False Personas:** you may develop 'masks' to cover your real self, you might smile a lot, always try to please others, appear self-confident and comfortable. You are convinced that others would despise you if they could see past your masks to your real self.

☐ **Perfectionism:** you reason that you will have nothing to feel ashamed about if you never make a mistake, and therefore you become a perfectionist. You do not accept your (or others') human imperfections.

☐ **Criticism/Judgment:** you attempt to throw off your painful shame feelings by becoming critical of everyone, making others appear flawed, ridiculous, stupid, idiotic, or uneducated. You become eager to point out the weaknesses of others, often leading to arrogance and self-judgment.

☐ **Rage:** you fight back against humiliation by attacking the supposed aggressor. By attacking you unconsciously defend your own fragile identity.

☐ Other:

_____

Describe how your defenses played out in this particular situation:

_____

_____

_____

B. **Challenge the shame:**

1. **Write the following affirmation at least three times:**

'**Even though I'm experiencing shame, like all humans I am worthy of love.**'

♥ _____

♥ _____

♥ _____

2. **My 'gifts' of this shame spiral are:**

(hint: the gifts of shame are often humility, containment, and humanity)

_____

_____

_____

3. Here are some examples of positive affirmations:

♥ I am a child of God and I deserve love, peace, prosperity, and serenity.

♥ I am loved because I deserve love.

♥ I forgive myself for hurting myself and others.

♥ I forgive myself for letting others hurt me.

♥ I forgive myself for accepting sex when I wanted love.

♥ I am not alone. I am one with God and the universe.

♥ I am whole and good.

♥ I am innocent and totally deserving of love unconditionally.

♥ I am capable of changing.

♥ Just for today, I will respect my own and other's boundaries.

♥ Just for today, I will be vulnerable with someone I can trust.

Write your own positive affirmation(s) at least three times:

♥ _____

♥ _____

♥ _____

♥ _____

♥ _____

♥ _____

♥ _____

♥ _____

♥ _____

♥ _____

♥ _____

♥ _____

♥ _____

4. **Repeat the affirmations over and over again until you believe them!!**

compass of shame

WITHDRAWING

- ☐ Covering your mouth with hand
- ☐ Biting your lower lip, stuttering
- ☐ Hiding in bed
- ☐ Wanting to crawl into a hole
- ☐ Wanting to shrink away after making a mistake
- ☐ Replaying painful events over and over in your mind
- ☐ Being overwhelmed, helpless
- ☐ Isolating hermit-like depression

N

ATTACKING OTHERS

- ☐ Judging others
- ☐ Criticizing others
- ☐ Belittling others
- ☐ Putting others down
- ☐ Blaming others
- ☐ Rejecting others
- ☐ Laughing at others
- ☐ Ridiculing others
- ☐ Lashing out physically

ATTACKING SELF

- ☐ Self-putdowns
- ☐ Self-ridicule
- ☐ Anger at yourself
- ☐ Self-blame
- ☐ Comparing self to others
- ☐ Self-contempt
- ☐ Masochism (pleasure in being humiliated — accepting shame in order to guarantee a link to others)

AVOIDING

- ☐ Perfectionism
- ☐ Preoccupation with image, plastic surgeries
- ☐ Pursuit of money, power, beauty, position
- ☐ Work, accomplishments
- ☐ Dissociation
- ☐ Grandiosity
- ☐ Failure to admit fault
- ☐ Thrill-seeking, sexual arousal, hedonism
- ☐ Addictions
- ☐ Denial

The four directions are highly damaging scripted behaviors that defend against shame. **Hiding, denying, pretending, distracting, or attacking** yourself or others to stuff your feelings can lead to isolation, masochism, addictions, explosive rage, or even extreme violence.

Adapted from the work of Donald L. Nathanson, MD and many others.

inheriting the family shame

a shame-based family environment **leads to** *shame-based personality characteristics*

☐ no affirmation	☐ low self-esteem
☐ performance over person	☐ human doing vs. human being
☐ scapegoating in family	☐ taking responsibility for everything
☐ anti-conflict family rules	☐ avoiding conflict
☐ no validation of effort	☐ self-doubt about my efforts
☐ cannot make mistakes	☐ perfectionism
☐ cannot do it right	☐ prone to failure
☐ must always do better	☐ over-achieving
☐ limited expressions of care	☐ desperate for approval
☐ conditional support	☐ others' opinions determine self-worth
☐ abandonment or neglect	☐ fear of abandonment
☐ attacking, hypercritical	☐ self-critical, self-hating
☐ unprocessed secrets	☐ fear of discovery / being caught
☐ extreme performance standards	☐ no effort is good enough
☐ emphasis on right or wrong	☐ categorical black-and-white thinking
☐ low 'us' concept	☐ heightened sense of unworthiness
☐ constriction of feelings	☐ unaware of feelings
☐ painful, unresolved issues	☐ tolerance of abuse
☐ needs denied, criticized	☐ conflicted needs
☐ personal limits not respected	☐ unhealthy or no boundaries

personal notes:

4. creating functional boundaries

What I value I will protect. What you value I will respect.
—Rokelle Lerner

I.   the purpose of boundaries

♦ **Your reality** is comprised of five components. These are:

1. **your body:** what you look like

2. **your thinking:** how you give meaning to incoming data

3. **your feelings:** your emotions

4. **your behavior:** what you do or do not do

5. **your spirituality:** your deep connection with your soul

♦ **Boundaries** control the impact of your reality on yourself and others. The purpose of a boundary is **to contain** and **protect** your sensory, cognitive, emotional, behavioral, and spiritual reality. Boundaries are a system of **setting limits** that enhance your **sense of self** and control how you **interact**: 'This is how far I shall go; this is what I will or won't do for you; this is what I won't tolerate from you.'

♦ **Boundaries are invisible, symbolic 'fences'** that keep people from coming into your space and abusing you and vice versa (emotionally, sexually, physically, psychologically, spiritually).

♦ Boundaries give you a way to **embody** your sense of 'who you are'.

♦ When your boundaries are in place, **they protect your thinking, feelings, physicality, and behavior** and enable you to **take responsibility** (be accountable). You **stop** blaming others for what you think, feel, and do. You also **stop** taking responsibility for the abusive feelings and behaviors of others. This allows you to **stop** manipulating / controlling those around you and to **stop** being manipulated / controlled by others.

♦ Without awareness of your own boundaries, you cannot be aware of or **sensitive to** the boundaries of others.

♦ **When boundaries are intact *and* flexible, you can have intimacy in your life**, but are protected against being abused physically, sexually, emotionally, intellectually, and spiritually.

♦ When you **do not** have functional boundaries, it is more likely that abuse and resentment may occur.

II. types of boundaries

- ◆ **External boundaries** protect your body by controlling who can touch you and how close they can be.

  - ♥ **Physical boundaries:** you determine when, where, how, and by whom you can be touched. You determine how close to you another person can stand.

  - ♥ **Sexual boundaries:** you determine where, when, how, and with whom you are sexual.

- ◆ **Internal boundaries** contain your thinking, feelings, and behavior and keep your interactions functional. You control what you think and feel and what you say and do or do not say and do. You control what you accept as true and have feelings about. This filtering system acts as a protective layer between you and others.

  - ♥ **Thinking boundaries** allow you to observe and control where you choose to focus your mind, avoiding distractions, internal 'noise', negative messages, and unwanted societal influences.

  - ♥ **Acting boundaries** allow you to focus your efforts on your personal priorities rather than on meeting the demands of others or the allure of self-sabotaging behaviors.

  - ♥ **Talking boundaries** provide personal containment, allowing you to speak clearly but diplomatically and share your emotions appropriately with moderation.

  - ♥ **Listening boundaries** allow you to sort through what others are saying and feeling and take in and have feelings about only what you know is true.

  Without an internal boundary you cannot hear who others are, hear what they think, or share who you are. Without an internal boundary others cannot hear who you are, hear what you think, or share who they are.

  Signs of *a lack* of internal boundaries are: sarcasm, blaming, judging, shaming, and controlling / manipulative behavior.

  When your internal boundary is *not* in place, you believe *you are responsible* for making someone feel, think, or do anything or vice versa.

  Two extremes: giving yourself permission to *tell others* what to think, feel, do, or not do, **OR** believing that you must *let others tell you* what to think, feel, do, or not do.

- ◆ **Three exceptions:**

  1. It is the parents' responsibility to **influence** their child's reality when the child exhibits dysfunctional behavior or thinking.

  2. It is the therapist's job to **tell a client** if his/her thinking, feeling, or behavior is skewed.

  3. When you ask someone for an opinion about your reality (sponsor, friend, or whomever), the person **has permission** to tell you.

III. signs of healthy boundaries (adapted from a lecture by Pia Mellody)

- ☐ Developing appropriate trust.
- ☐ Revealing a little of yourself at a time, then checking to see how the other person responds to your sharing.
- ☐ Moving step by step into intimacy.
- ☐ Putting a new acquaintanceship 'on hold' until you check for compatibility.
- ☐ Deciding whether a potential relationship will be good for you.
- ☐ Staying focused on your own growth and recovery.
- ☐ Weighing the consequences before you act on sexual impulses.
- ☐ Enjoying your sexual feelings by focusing largely on your own pleasure rather than on monitoring your partner's reactions.
- ☐ Maintaining your personal values despite what others may want.
- ☐ Noticing when someone else displays inappropriate boundaries.
- ☐ Noticing when someone invades your boundaries.
- ☐ Saying 'NO' to food, gifts, touch, or sex you don't want.
- ☐ Asking a person before touching them.
- ☐ Respecting others—not taking advantage of someone's generosity.
- ☐ Developing self-respect—not giving too much in hope that someone will like you.
- ☐ Not allowing someone to take advantage of your generosity.
- ☐ Trusting your own decisions.
- ☐ Defining your truth as you see it.
- ☐ Knowing who you are and what you want.
- ☐ Recognizing that friends and partners are not mind readers.
- ☐ Clearly communicating your wants and needs (and recognizing that you may be turned down, but you *can* ask).
- ☐ Becoming your own loving parent.
- ☐ Talking with yourself with gentleness, humor, love, and respect.

IV. codependence perpetuates unhealthy boundaries

♦ **Four kinds of impaired boundaries** result from experiencing less-than-nurturing parenting/caregiving:

♥ **No Boundaries** allow no protection. Having no sense of being abused or being abusive and/or having trouble saying 'No' or protecting yourself, you allow others to take advantage of you.

♥ **Damaged Boundaries** give partial protection. A damaged boundary system has 'holes' in it. At times or with certain people you can say 'No' and set limits, and at other times or with other people you cannot. Pay close attention to boundary issues when you are Hungry, Angry, Lonely, or Tired [**HALT!**]. (Mellody 15)

♥ **A system of Walls** offers complete protection but no intimacy. Anger or niceness; silence or words (continuing to talk even when someone politely tries to contribute); fear (retreat from others); observing rather than participating.

♥ **Moving Back and Forth** between Walls and No Boundaries. Dropping the 'walls' and risking being **too** vulnerable makes you feel undefended when you have an experience of no boundaries.

♦ Whenever you don't have good boundaries, **you can't tell where your reality starts and someone else's reality begins** (the individuation/differentiation process). Your reality blends with the other person's, and you believe you can tell the other person how to think, feel, and behave because he/she is an extension of you. You read the other person's thoughts and feelings and choose your behavior based on your perceptions of the other person's opinions of you. This is also called **enmeshment**.

♦ **Intimacy is blocked** in a relationship when you are being victimized because of your impaired boundaries.

♦ **Substance dependence and other compulsive/impulsive behaviors** disregard your limits. They push and step boldly across your boundaries. You give in. You move your boundaries back until you tolerate things you said you would never tolerate and do things you said you would never do. (Beattie 218)

♦ Your *increased tolerance* of inappropriate behaviors may reverse. You may become totally *intolerant* of even the most human behaviors. In the beginning you make excuses for a person's inappropriate behavior, and toward the end there is no excuse. (Ibid.)

♦ You not only tolerate unhealthy and inappropriate behaviors, but eventually you may convince yourself **these behaviors are normal** and **what you deserve**. (Ibid.)

♦ These unhealthy boundaries become so familiar that **you don't even recognize when these things are happening**. This pattern becomes so pervasive that it becomes **unconscious**. (Ibid.)

♦ Living with **subtle problems** such as a non-drinking alcoholic who is not in recovery can be more difficult than the more blatant behaviors. You sense something is wrong and **start feeling** *crazy*. You can't understand why because you **can't or won't** accept your reality. (Ibid.)

42

V. boundary violations in sexual abuse

♦ Where there is dependence and a **power imbalance**, there is no autonomy, and thus no true consent, even if there is acquiescence.

♦ Child sexual abuse and incest are unlawful behaviors with **severe consequences** for victims, perpetrators, and their families. They are also **extreme boundary violations** that inflict serious harm on all involved.

♦ **Survivors** of child sexual abuse may experience stigma, somatic symptoms, emotional constriction, a lack of trust, a controlling interpersonal style, damaged relationships with family members, a lack of sexual boundaries, and repeating the cycle of sexual abuse.

♦ **Symbiosis** is defined as the interaction of two organisms that mutually depend on each other: for example, a blind person and his/her guide dog.

♦ Enmeshed or **symbiotic families** enforce **mutual codependence**, suffocate individual selfhood, and lack the personal and intergenerational boundaries that protect the **separate identity** and **roles** of both children and adult caregivers.

♦ To meet parental needs, vulnerable children are **blackmailed emotionally** and coaxed into **role reversals**: shopping, cooking, cleaning, caring for younger siblings and impaired caregivers, containing emotions, and mediating conflicts. They crave attention and are led to believe that *to earn parental love* they must meet the emotional needs and/or sexual demands of symbiotic adults for covert (emotional) or overt incest. (Weinhold 193)

♦ **Sexual abuse** is an outcome of both dysfunctional family boundaries and the incomplete developmental processes of **codependence**. The narcissistic adult expects the child to provide nurture, love, affection, comfort, and protection lacking in an adult relationship. This leads to sexualizing their **symbiotic enmeshment**.

♦ The adult uses the child sexually to ritualize a grandiose fantasy of symbiotic union. Their identities are fused in intense mutual dependence. The child may cling to the perpetrator, fear abandonment, threats, and loss of self, or become seductive with adults. Separation or failure can trigger depression, rage, guilt, and violent explosions. The child may repeat the pattern as an adult abuser or prostitute.

♦ A destructive symbiotic adult has experienced insufficient secure bonding and is unable to be separate with functioning boundaries. This creates strong needs for warmth, closeness, acceptance, and intimacy. A person who has not had these experiences is unable to verbalize these needs. He or she yearns to be close to someone—to be held/touched. (Ibid.)

♦ Strong fears of abandonment make it too risky or scary to fulfill these needs with adults. The warmth and innocence of the child soothes these fears and creates the safety necessary for the adult's unmet narcissistic needs. (Ibid.)

♦ When a destructively symbiotic father turns to his daughter for sex in an unconscious attempt to meet his developmental needs, he is seldom aware of what he actually needs. Most people who commit incest are completely out of touch with their needs and feelings and have no experience in meeting them in healthy ways. (Weinhold 195)

♦ These adults regress to an infantile state in which their own needs/feelings are regarded as most important. They do not know how to be close to a child and affectionate in a non-sexual way, to meet their own needs, to belong, or to have a warm relationship in a non-physical way. Hence they try to sexualize most of their relationships. (Ibid. 193)

VI. reclaiming functional boundaries

♦ **Boundaries must be taught**. Very small children have no boundaries, no internal way to protect themselves from abuse or to avoid being abusive toward others. The parents' responsibility is to protect them from abuse and respectfully confront their children's own abusive behavior. This **protection/confrontation** eventually teaches the children to have healthy, firm, but flexible boundaries by the time they reach adulthood. (Mellody 14)

♦ You need to **learn to set limits** on what you shall do to and for people, and what you will allow people to do to and for you. (Beattie 218)

♦ People you relate to **need to know** you have boundaries. You need to inform them; that is your responsibility. (Ibid.)

♦ You are advised against inflexibility but need to **understand your limits**. (Ibid. 219)

♦ As you grow and change, you **may want or need to change your boundaries**.

♦ **Examples of setting boundaries:** (Ibid.)

☐ I will not allow anyone to physically/verbally abuse me.

☐ I will not knowingly believe or support lies.

☐ I will not allow chemical abuse or criminal behavior in my home.

☐ I will not lie to protect you or me from your substance use.

☐ If you want to act crazy that's your business, but you can't do it in front of me. Either you leave or I'll walk away.

☐ I will not use my home as a detoxification center for recovering substance users.

☐ I will not finance a person's substance use or other irresponsible behavior.

☐ I will not rescue people from the consequences of their alcohol/drug abuse or other irresponsible behavior.

☐ You can spoil your fun, your day, your life—that's your business. But I won't let you spoil my fun, my day, or my life!

♦ **Clues to some boundaries you need to set:** (Ibid.)

☐ Things you're sick of, can't stand, or make threats about:

☐ Others:

- People may **get angry** with you for setting boundaries: they can't use you anymore. They may try to make you **feel guilty** so you will remove your boundary. You will be **tested** to see if you're serious, especially if you haven't meant what you said in the past. **Empty threats** will reduce your credibility. (Ibid. 219-20)

- Setting limits/boundaries takes time and effort. **Stick to your boundaries and enforce them.** Be consistent. (Ibid.)

- Watch your **tolerance level** so that the pendulum doesn't swing too far to either extreme (no boundary vs. wall). (Ibid.)

- If others act abusively or **transgress** your boundaries (for whatever reason) and are **not** willing to establish and maintain boundaries for themselves, you can **discern**

    - ♥ whom you **choose** to be with and what type of organizations you want to **affiliate** with.
    - ♥ the type and amount of **information** you share.
    - ♥ how much **time** (if any) to spend with those people and what type of **activities** to do with them. (Mellody 50)

- While talking/listening, use your internal boundary to make **clear 'I' statements**.

- Practice maintaining functional boundaries every day in every interaction. You will not do this perfectly. Practice makes better.

VII. using internal boundaries in communication (adapted from Pia Mellody)

- Establishing clear communication with others begins with your internal self-talk. Through conscious practice you are developing both clear **talking boundaries** and sensitive **listening boundaries**. These are **intentional 'filters'** that protect others from misunderstanding what you say and protect yourself from misunderstanding what you hear others say.

- Here are some ways to improve your speaking and listening:

    1. Use your internal boundary to clarify your intention for speaking. What is the **core truth** about your experience that you are **willing to share**, stripped of any confusing emotional baggage?

    2. Regardless of the immediate emotional dynamics in your situation, stay attuned to your connection with **your deepest self** and in tune with your connection with other listeners in the conversation.

    3. Set aside any **impulsive reactions**: to blame, shame, judge, demean, guilt-trip, control, or manipulate anyone (use these as internal clues to your emotional state).

    4. Breathe consciously to **stay present** in your body and with your emotions.

    5. Speak clearly, concisely, and honestly, **limiting yourself** to reporting what happened (facts), what it means to you and others (possible interpretations), and how you responded (personal feelings and acts).

6. **Take ownership** of your interpretations, acts, and feelings without blaming others or yourself. If your responses have recently changed or if you would prefer to change them, say so.

7. Ask for feedback from your listener(s) to **confirm** that the message you sent was the message received. Do you feel 'heard'?

8. Intentionally set aside an agreed-upon amount of time to **listen deeply** to what others want to say to you.

9. When others are speaking, use your internal boundary to listen for what is **true**, what is **untrue**, and what is **questionable**.

10. Do not let yourself **get defensive, feel shamed, or take the blame** because of what anyone else says to (or about) you.

11. Listen for the truth about **who the other person is**, not simply to counter his/her point of view with your own arguments.

12. As you listen deeply to what others are saying, notice and learn to self-regulate your emotional state by **breathing consciously**.

13. If what you are hearing is **true**, allow yourself to feel your authentic emotional response.

14. If you notice that you are getting angry or anxious or frustrated, it's OK to **acknowledge** that at an appropriate point by making a carefully non-judgmental 'I statement' that discloses what you are noticing about your feeling state.

15. When you succeed at owning and sharing your authentic emotional truth in a safe, non-blaming way, your listeners can feel their **connection with you** more deeply.

16. If what you are hearing is **NOT true**, notice any feelings that come up but remember that 'This is **NOT** about me' and be careful **NOT** to own them by getting defensive, hostile, or vindictive.

17. If what you are hearing is **questionable**, you may ask for clarification (more information/data) to make a determination. Be succinct, objective, non-argumentative, and non-blaming.

♦ The essence of clear communication is **NOT** to vent your emotions, achieve agreement, or force sameness. It is developing a mutual understanding of both your different perspectives and your underlying connectedness.

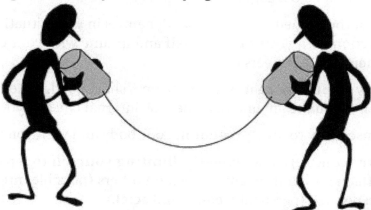

VIII. experiential exercises

1. **Questions to explore:**

    ♥ What are some boundaries you've set early in your recovery?

    ♥ What are some boundaries you've set recently?

    ♥ Can you remember how you felt before and after you set that boundary?

    ♥ Were you called on to enforce it?

    ♥ What are the most difficult kind of boundaries for you to set and enforce?

    ♥ How do you feel when you're around people with rigid boundaries—too many rules and regulations?

    ♥ How do you feel when you're around people with few or no boundaries?

    ♥ Is somebody in your life now using you or not treating you appropriately or respectfully?

    ♥ Are you now complaining, angry, whining, or upset about something?

    ♥ What's preventing you from taking care of yourself?

    ♥ What do you think will happen if you do?

    ♥ What do you think will happen if you don't?

    ♥ In the past, what have you been willing to lose for the sake of a particular relationship?

    ♥ What are you willing to lose now?

    ♥ What are you **not** willing to lose?

2. **Physical boundaries/comfort zone exercise**

    Have individuals pair up, line up across the room, ask them to take a step, check in with own reality/comfort level, ask them to take another step, etc., until partners find a comfortable distance for them both. Now take another step closer and notice any discomfort. What comes up? Move back into their comfort zone and check in with their own reality.

3. **Dyad exercise: talking/listening boundaries**

    One person speaks for 3 minutes; the other only listens to understand. Then listener spends a few minutes repeating back, 'What I heard you say was...' without feedback. Now switch.

4. **Identify boundary violations and come up with solutions.**

boundary violations

physical boundary violations:

- Hitting
- Touching in any way without permission
- Invading one's space, materials, belongings
- Standing too close without permission
- Not allowing privacy in bedroom or bath
- Opening/reading mail, diaries, journals
- Smoking around nonsmokers in non-smoking areas
- Exposing others to contagious disease
- Eavesdropping

sexual boundary violations:

- Forcing any sexual activity, even with a committed partner
- Demanding unsafe sexual practices with a partner
- Exposing oneself or sexual behavior without permission
- Overt public sexuality
- Staring or looking lustfully
- Sexual jokes or innuendo
- Leaving pornography around
- Comments about one's body or appearance
- Sexually shaming another person

internal boundary violations:

- Attempting to control another
- Discounting another's reality
- Shaming, humiliating
- Raging: yelling, name-calling, cursing
- Belittling
- Interrupting
- Interrogating
- Lying, deceiving, betraying
- Sarcasm
- Joking about or laughing at
- Patronizing
- Violating a confidence
- Giving unsolicited advice
- Asking personal or sexual questions
- Blaming, judging, or criticizing
- Gossiping
- Breaking a commitment for no reason

signs of boundary damage

signs of damaged physical boundaries:

- Inability to say 'No' to physical contact
- Allowing someone to stand in your face (or too close)
- Touching someone without asking
- Accepting food or gifts you don't want
- Not noticing boundary violations
- Allowing yourself to be abused
- Self-abuse
- Food abuse

signs of damaged sexual boundaries:

- Inability to say 'No' to sexual contact
- Projecting your desires onto someone else
- Answering sexual questions
- Being sexual for your partner, not yourself
- Unsafe sexual practices
- Acting on first sexual impulse
- Going against your values to please partner
- Sexual abuse

signs of damaged internal boundaries:

- Telling all, right away.
- Answering for another person
- Needing to explain your behavior
- Accepting blame for others' feelings
- Assuming you can mind-read
- Accepting authority unquestioningly
- Believing anyone and everyone
- Allowing others to direct your life, define your reality
- Expecting others to anticipate or fill your needs
- Allowing someone to take as much as they can from you.
- Letting others direct your life
- Letting others define you
- Believing others can anticipate your needs
- Feeling upset so someone will take care of you

personal external boundaries assessment

1. In what circumstances (when/with whom) do you experience these four **physical** and **sexual** boundary conditions?
2. How do you feel and how do you behave when you have that boundary experience?

External boundaries include your physical and sexual boundaries

Boundary Condition	Circumstances (when or with whom it exists)	Feeling/Behavior (what you feel/how you behave)	Consequences (what are the results?)
No Boundary			
Wall			
Damaged Boundary			
Functional Boundary			

personal internal boundaries assessment

1. In what circumstances (when/with whom) do you experience these four internal boundary conditions?
2. How do you feel and how do you behave when you have that boundary experience?

Internal boundaries include your thoughts, feelings, intentions, listening / talking

Boundary Condition	Circumstances (when or with whom it exists)	Feeling/Behavior (what you feel/how you behave)	Consequences (what are the results?)
No Boundary			
Wall			
Damaged Boundary			
Functional Boundary			

OUCH!

NO LISTENING
BOUNDARY

GREAT!

5. effective communication

Effective communication builds a bridge connecting people's lives more intimately. When we are truly talking and listening to one another, doors between us open, allowing each into the other's world. Improving our communication skills will assist us in living more happily and in creating greater connection with ourselves and with others. —paraphrased from Richard S., *Communication Skills*

I.   developing communication skills

♦ No one is born with excellent communication skills; you **develop** them as you do language skills. As a child you depended upon your parents and other adults to **model effective communication**.

♦ Normal development of communication skills may be **disrupted** in dysfunctional family systems (where substance/process addictions are active, where mental illness is present, or where parents are self-absorbed as a result of unresolved trauma issues).

♦ **Ineffective communication** (manipulating, people-pleasing, controlling, blaming, covering up, lying) fails to bring people together.

♦ Ineffective communication **reeks** of repressed feelings, repressed thoughts, ulterior motives, low self-worth, shame. There is a tendency to react inappropriately and subsequently move into a defensive position.

♦ Effective communication requires daily attention and **mindfulness**.

♦ Effective communication allows for the **exchange** of important information.

♦ Effective communication allows you to inform others about **who you are and what you want** (i.e. to share your reality).

♦ Without effective communication, there cannot be **intimacy**.

II.   how codependence affects communication

♦ **When you are out of touch with yourself** and have experienced insufficient nurturing around your connectedness, you will lean towards either becoming dependent upon others or becoming anti-dependent. When you believe that others have all the answers, you will feel angry, hurt, scared, guilty, needy, and/or controlled.

♦ **Knowing who you are** is something you aspire to establish and maintain: that who you are is OK, that your feelings/thoughts are OK, that your opinions count, that it is OK to talk/discuss your problems, that it is OK to say 'No' ('No' is a complete sentence).

♦ **When you have difficulty containing yourself,** you will tend to lean toward being out of control or controlling of others.

51

♦ **When you have difficulty esteeming yourself from within**, you tend to value pleasing others at any cost. You do this for '**other esteem**'. In addition, you will also tend to fear disapproval and abandonment. When you are able to esteem yourself from within, you will be able to and are impelled to talk clearly and openly.

♦ **When you are disconnected from your soul**, you tend to hope for everything, but believe **you deserve nothing**. Thus the difficulty you may experience in manifesting work positions/situations that nurture you.

III. practicing your communication skills

♦ Assertiveness is the **ground** between submissiveness and aggressiveness.

♦ **Be assertive** (stand up for yourself) without being abrasive/aggressive.

♦ Being assertive allows you to communicate in ways that enable you to maintain your self-respect, pursue your goals, satisfy your needs, and defend your rights and personal space without **diminishing or manipulating** others.

♦ A person who is assertive stands up for his or her **rights** and expresses personal needs, values, concerns, and ideas in **direct** and appropriate ways.

♦ **Listening** is the most neglected element of effective communication.

♦ For some people listening may require **more effort** than talking. Try listening carefully for a selected time.

♦ Effective communication requires **two people listening and talking in turn**. Interrupting others is disrespectful and easily frustrates people.

♦ What you understand a person is saying may **not** be what he or she **means**. **Check it out:** 'This is what I heard you say, is that accurate?' You might also check out what the other person **thinks** you have said.

♦ **Ask for time to talk:** request time to speak.

♦ **Ask questions:** question like you would like to be questioned, with respect and kindness.

♦ **Agree to disagree:** signal major concerns to each other and identify your areas of disagreement. Be as detailed and specific as you can. In many instances, agreeing about your differences is already a success.

♦ **Compliment the other person** for expressing himself or herself well. Tell the person what you most appreciate. Make a list of effective communication skills that you admire in others.

♦ **Do not attack the way others communicate:** don't tell the person how THEY are feeling.

♦ **Don't judge others' communication style:** 'You're being too sensitive.' 'The therapist said you shouldn't be so blaming...'

♦ **Don't take another person's inventory:** focusing on another person's behavior rather than your own is disrespectful, dysfunctional, and not very useful.

- **'Own' your behavior:** quoting outsiders brings into the conversation a third party who really shouldn't be there (authorities, books, friends, newspaper articles to justify your point of view). In doing this, you are saying 'See, I'm right, even my friend Betty thinks you are not being very honest about this'.

- **Give up having to be right:** in any given conversation, ask yourself: 'What is my intention?' Is your intention to create greater connection, to clarify your position on a topic, to be divisive, or what?

- **Show compassion/concern without rescuing:** 'Sounds like you are having a problem. What do you need from me? I'm sorry you are having a problem!'

- **Discuss feelings/problems without expecting to be rescued!** Early in life you learned that it was wrong to talk about problems; that it was wrong to express feelings; that it was wrong to express opinions and/or to have different opinions.

- In effective communication, **say what you mean and mean what you say.**

- If you don't know, say **'I don't know!'**

- **Be concise:** get to the point and stop!

- **Share secrets with friends:** discern with whom, how much, and the best time.

- **Express feelings** openly, honestly, appropriately, and responsibly: learn the words 'I feel...'

- **Listen to hear the other person's reality without thinking of what you will say.**

- **Do not try to fix people!**

- **Say what you expect** without demanding that others change. Likewise, you don't have to change to suit them.

- **Do not give advice/suggestions** unless solicited.

- **Learn to express your wants and needs:** which requires that you discern what your wants and needs are ...

- **Speak your truth:** remember, it is the WHOLE truth that sets you free. It's not polite to withhold telling your truth. It is being emotionally dishonest, which is a form of abandonment. In love and in dignity, speak your truth—what you think, feel, your actions, what you know—and it shall set you free.

- **Do not allow other people to control you and vice versa.** Control can take the forms of guilt-tripping, coercion, force, etc. When you establish healthy boundaries, you can stop participating in controlling behavior.

- **Ignore nonsense.** You can say 'I don't want to discuss this!'

- **Settle into being listened to!**

- **Take responsibility** for how you communicate. Use words that reflect a high **self-esteem** along with **esteem** for others.

- **Be direct and firm.**

- **Be gentle and loving.**

IV. resolving conflict (adapted from Arnold Mindell's work)

1. **Process conflicts when they arise.** Your first inclination may be to avoid conflicts. Do not wait until they become unnecessarily polarized.

    ♥ Keep in mind that inner and outer conflict is **normal** and **inevitable**. It is a sign of **self-balance** and of development and **growth**.

    ♥ **Within conflict** lies the potential for growth and self-discovery.

    ♥ Conflict is not only an expression of your own troubles, complexes, or personal psychology. It can also be a **combination** of internal tensions, relationship troubles, and group and world problems.

    ♥ For a community, conflict is **useful** in order to understand itself and realize its full potential.

2. **Notice the conflict.** Signals of conflict include: verbal disagreement, lack of overt communication, remaining separate by space or time, gossiping about the opponent, having bad dreams or fantasies about the opponent, or being suspicious or mistrustful of the opponent.

3. **Conflicts can be minor or severe. A conflict needs to be worked on** when the problem is festering, is producing bad feelings, and is increasing over time; people have been gossiping for a long time; it's malevolent and includes an increasing number of people; the problem never resolves itself and ruins the atmosphere whereby people want to stay away; you avoid the problem because of hopelessness or lack of courage.

4. **Getting involved in the conflict:** What is your reason for **not** entering into the conflict? What or whom are you afraid of? (Experiment with being this person.) Is your fear due to loss of awareness during fights? Do you become unconscious, dizzy, or moody?

5. **Set up a time and place both parties agree upon.** If your partner does not appear, then you may work on the problem internally. Ask opponent if he/she is willing to work on problem. Ask if he/she agrees to work on it. If the person does not want to work on it, ask if they have an idea on how to resolve the conflict. If the solution is not useful, ask if they would consider a facilitator. If this approach is revoked, take the conflict internally and try to resolve it there.

6. **Processing awareness:** a conflict has several states: neutral, on the other person's side, or on your own side. It only requires you to be aware, not to change your opponent.

7. **Taking your own side:** discern your feelings (remember, what you feel may be part of the whole energy field that is not sufficiently expressed). In such a case you are serving others. Feel the emotions and express them to yourself. Try to accept these states. Report your inner experiences: what do you notice? What are your feelings, images, and experiences?

8. **De-escalating to neutrality:** maybe because you feel sorry for your partner, maybe because you are being too one sided, maybe because you no longer fully agree with yourself, once you take your own side, chances are that you will de-escalate, quieting your voice, moving away, looking away, or simply losing interest. When people get

stuck in their viewpoints, it is usually because they have not completely expressed them or have become attached to and identified with them and have lost awareness of their de-escalating signals.

9. **Taking your partner's position:** this will work only if it is genuine. If you cannot do this, try to determine whether you are still on your side or if you are feeling neutral. Use your compassion to help your opponent express his position better. Try to imagine the feelings your opponent is having. Check the feedback from your opponent.

   Remember that you come into conflict with others because of parts of yourself that you, like your opponent, are unconsciously upset about.

10. **Cycling:** after taking your side, the side of neutrality, and your partner's side, the cycles enter into a new level. New issues, new reactions, or new feelings come up. If you do not know your feelings or feel unconscious or incongruent, step into the neutral position. The conflict may be incomplete because you did not fully express the feelings on your side, or did not fully understand your partner's position.

    Use your awareness to see if there is a slight moment of relaxation, a flicker of a smile, a small sigh of relief. If so, let it go. Remember to consider the conflicting sides as two inner parts of themselves that are asking for individual resolution.

    If you get stuck on your side, you may not have been able to complete the real feelings you have, or you have been hurt by the other and cannot express your hurt and anger.

11. No one wins a conflict unless both feel understood and enlightened about the theme or the nature of the other. Enlightenment is a field experience: unless all feel enlightened, no one feels enlightened.

12. After working through a conflict, ask yourself:

    ♥ What did I need and/or want from the person?

    ♥ What did I get from the interaction?

    ♥ Did I ask clearly for what I needed/wanted?

    ♥ Was I able to ask clearly without making demands or threats?

    ♥ Were we able to negotiate differences?

    ♥ Were we able to take each other's side?

    ♥ Did either one of us hurt the other person?

    ♥ Did I learn something new about my partner or about myself?

    ♥ Did I reveal something new about myself to my partner?

    ♥ What would I do differently?

    ♥ Did we end up feeling closer at the conclusion?

13. Confrontation quickly engages the confronter and the confrontee in interaction. Confront only people you want to get closer to or people who are invading your space without your permission.

V. conflict resolution checklist (adapted from Arnold Mindell's work)

A. Problem Definition:

☐ Mutual Ownership ('We have a problem.')

☐ Brief Description ('Here is *an* example of what I mean.')

☐ Present and Future Oriented ('Perhaps the next time we...')

☐ Issue Level, not Personality Level ('The *issue* seems to be...')

☐ Issue Agreed On ('It sounds like you and I agree on the problem.')

B. Problem Resolution:

☐ Listen (Observe, acknowledge, don't interrupt.)

☐ Check it out ('Let me see if I understand.')

☐ Validate ('I see how you could feel that way.')

☐ Brainstorm ('Let's think of some possible options.')

☐ Positive presentation ('I would appreciate it if...')

☐ Compromise ('If you would..., I would be willing to...')

☐ Agree ('Sounds like we have agreed to try...')

☐ Repeat ('Let me make sure I understand what we have agreed to...')

☐ Congratulate ('We did a good job. Let's take a break.')

VI. feedback wheel (adapted from Pia Mellody's work)

1. Describe the problem/behavior objectively (When you....).

2. Share your feelings about the problem ('I feel....').

3. Describe the effects/results or the 'need' you have ('I want to...' **OR** 'Because I have a need for...').

4. Listen to the other person's feedback about the conflict and reflect back what you heard him/her say ('What I hear you say was...').

5. Describe clearly what you want from the other person in a clear request ('What I want from you is for you to....' 'Would you be willing to...?').

6. Negotiate any differences between what you want and what the other person is willing to give or do ('I need to be able to let off steam when I feel angry. I would like to be able to raise my voice'... 'Well, I can handle your raised voice if it doesn't turn into yelling and screaming and if you don't direct it at me.').

VII. reflective listening

1. **Respect and commitment:** You have to care enough about yourself and others to want to work it out.

2. **Dealing with feelings:** Ask yourself: 'What's really going on?' Have the courage to get honest with yourself: 'I feel _____.'

3. **Reflective listening:** From respect to understanding ... listening for feelings. Your goal here is to make the other person feel understood (**not** to express your point of view or defend yourself).

Examples:
'It sounds like you're feeling frustrated with me because I don't seem to listen.'
OR *'What I hear you saying is that you get upset with me when I don't listen.'*
OR *'So you feel annoyed when I don't listen to you...'*

VIII. experiential exercises

♦ **Have people pair up and have a five-minute conversation** with each other. One listens while the other is talking. Before switching, make sure each person clearly understands and/or reflects back what the other was communicating.

♦ **If unable to negotiate differences in a relationship, agree to disagree.** If differences are irresolvable and the relationship ends, make it a ceremony of completion. Write a letter stating your perception of the irresolvable differences without blame, seeing yourself and the other as okay.

♦ **Question: Why are you afraid to tell others who you are?** Keep in mind that the words you speak reflect who you are, what you think, judge, feel, value, honor, hate, fear, desire, hope for, believe in, commit to ...

☐ Fear of rejection?

☐ Not sure who you are or what you want to say?

☐ Don't believe it's okay to be who you are?

☐ Don't like or trust yourself?

☐ Fear of attack (physical, intellectual, emotional)?

♦ **Conflict Resolution Exercise**

1. Choose a partner.

2. Describe a real conflict with a real opponent you have in your life right now.

3. Have your partner play the opponent.

4. Take your own side strongly.

5. Take the side of your opponent strongly.

6. Notice when you are uncomfortable with your position and either become neutral or take your opponent's side.

7. Go back to your original role and notice if things have changed or continue until the conflict disappears.

6. your emotional reality

Difficulty owning your emotional reality stems from having your experience ignored, attacked, and/or having it denied or disputed. This is experienced in two ways: (1) 'I know and I don't or won't tell', or (2) 'I don't know'.

I. avoiding your feelings

♦ The dominator model of social organization has emphasized the importance of developing your left-brain hemisphere that comprises your **logical, rational, and linear** thinking functions while **de-emphasizing** your right brain that comprises your **creative, non-linear, feeling** functions. Consequently, you may be completely out of touch with your creativity and wouldn't know a feeling if it bit you on the nose.

♦ You may **use words as feelings**, and these often become ways to **avoid** having your feelings or to **justify** your behavior.

☐ Words like 'I am **frustrated**, I am **annoyed**, or I am **irritated**' usually cover **anger**.

☐ Words like 'I am **confused**, I am **uneasy**, or I am **tense**' cover **fear**.

☐ Words like 'I am **lonely**, I am **bored**, I am **empty**, or I am **low**' cover **pain**.

☐ Some words represent a combination of feelings: 'I am **depressed**, I am **unhappy**, or I am **upset**' can be a **combination** of anger, fear, and/or pain.

☐ 'I am **suffering**' usually signals anger and fear when you do not have permission to **express** these emotions.

♦ If you grew up in a **dysfunctional** family system:

☐ you were systematically taught to **inhibit** and suppress your feelings.

☐ you were talked out of your feelings and taught to **distrust** what you felt and/or to trust only what others told you they were feeling.

☐ you did not get your **emotional needs** met by your caregivers.

☐ you did not have your feelings **listened to**, forcing you to deal with your feelings alone. You built defenses against feeling your feelings, trying to shut them out of your awareness, which helped you to survive your childhood. But as a result, you have become totally **out of touch** with your emotions.

II. what are feelings and what is their function?

♦ Feelings are natural, **normal** responses to your experiences.

♦ Feelings are **not** good or bad, right or wrong, positive or negative.

- Feelings are emotional energy. You have feelings; you **are not** your feelings.

- Feelings can help you form your **values** and make decisions.

- Without awareness of your feelings, you **lose** the fullness and richness of your life.

- Feelings are **indicators**:

  - ♥ when you feel happy, comfortable, warm and content, you usually know **all is well** in your world for the present.

  - ♥ Likewise, with **anger, fear or sadness**. Your feelings of anger can motivate you to **solve** a bothersome problem; fear may encourage you to **protect** yourself and/or to remove yourself from dangerous situations/people; repeated hurt and emotional pain tells you to **stay away**.

- Feelings can provide you with **clues** to yourself: your desires, needs, ambitions.

- Feelings assist you to discover yourself: what you are *really* thinking.

- Your feelings connect you to the **deep** part of yourself that seeks and knows truth and desires self-preservation, self-enhancement, safety, and goodness.

- Your feelings are connected to your instinct and **intuition**.

- If you don't feel your feelings and deal with them responsibly, they will **control** you.

- Your feelings are your own. **Nobody makes anyone feel.** No one is ultimately responsible for your feelings except for you, no matter how much you insist they are.

  - ♥ Other people might *help* you feel, but they don't *make* you feel.

  - ♥ You are responsible for *choosing* to be considerate of other people's feelings.

  - ♥ People cannot change the way you feel. Only you can do that!

- Your feelings are **reactions** to life's circumstances. Thus: 'I feel such and such when you do such and such because...' **NOT** 'You *made* me feel...'

- Your feelings **tell you** a great deal about yourself and your relationships.

- Dealing with your feelings requires a **change** in your thinking. **What you think** influences how you feel.

- Sometimes inaccurate, overactive, or inappropriate **thought patterns cause emotions** or cause them to remain longer than necessary.

- After you feel your emotions, it is important that you **examine your thinking**.

- Sharing that emotional part of yourself with others creates **closeness and intimacy**.

- If you want an intimate relationship with someone, you need to discuss your present feelings with them; this develops **emotional intimacy**.

- Suppressed emotional feelings cause **obsessive/compulsive behavior**.

- Suppressed emotions also lead to **resentment**, which leads to rage.

- Suppressed feelings cause **system dysfunction**, which can manifest as mental, emotional, and physical disease.

III. maladaptive ways of being with your feelings

☐ **Crying** when you need to get angry.

☐ Getting **angry** to cover up your fear, sadness, or hurt.

☐ Getting **depressed** instead of taking action.

☐ **Blaming** your feelings on others ('You made me angry, sad' etc.) in order to get your feelings out.

☐ Believing that expressing certain feelings is a sign of **your weakness** (men don't cry, women shouldn't get angry).

☐ Letting others' feelings **control** your thoughts, feelings, and actions.

☐ Letting your thoughts **block** your feelings or your feelings **block** your thoughts.

☐ Giving **more power** to your feelings than they deserve: 'If I started crying, I would never be able to stop', or 'If I get angry, I will hurt someone'.

☐ Believing your feelings are bad and should be **avoided**. As a result, you may become addicted to a substance or activity to **avoid feeling anything**.

☐ Believing that your happy feelings **must** be followed by sad feelings because this is the way it usually was in your family of origin.

IV. being emotionally present is healing

♦ Make **awareness of yourself** a habit. Develop your 'observer self'.

♦ **Listen** to what you are thinking and saying, your tone of voice.

♦ **Being emotionally present** is about **not** censoring, blocking, or running from your feelings. Don't tell yourself: 'Don't feel that!'

♦ **Experience** your feelings as fully as possible when they surface. **Allow** their emotional energy to pass through your body.

♦ **Realize** that you can think and feel at the same time, and then do it!

♦ **Identify** each separate feeling, and don't use one to block another.

♦ Deal with having your feelings. **Examine** the thoughts that go with each feeling and accept them without suppression or censorship.

♦ Don't **pass judgment** on yourself for your feelings.

♦ Decide **what**, if anything, you want to do about your feelings and the accompanying thoughts.

♦ Evaluate the situation; then **choose a behavior** in line with your moral code and your new ideal of self-care. Ask yourself: 'Is there a problem I need to solve?' and 'Is my thinking off-base?'

♦ Is the problem something you **can** solve? Does it concern another person? Is it necessary or appropriate to **discuss** the feeling with that person? If so, **when**? Sometimes waiting is important: detaching, waiting a day or two ...

- Being emotionally present will take **practice** and awareness.

- Physical exercise, writing letters you don't intend to send, talking to people you feel safe with, and quiet time in meditation all will assist you to **access your feelings.**

- Own your feelings and take responsibility for **being the source** of your feelings.

- **Recognize** your feelings, and don't use them to manipulate others.

- Stay current in the **expression** of your feelings, and don't store them up.

- Embrace your feelings as your **friends and allies** that give you information, rather than as **enemies** to be avoided.

- Remember that there are **no 'bad' feelings**, and that there is an **important purpose** for each feeling. Identify that purpose and learn from it.

V.   four kinds of feeling reality

- **Adult Feeling Reality** involves experiencing mature, authentic emotional responses to your thinking reality. They help you to feel centered and connected within. Your current thinking about your life today creates these feelings.

- **Adult Induced Feeling Reality** is the result of a process called **empathy**. This results when:

   ♥ you place yourself in another's shoes.

   ♥ another person is in denial or is irresponsible about his/her feelings.

   Empathy becomes a problem when you take in too much (or feel too intensely) and become **overwhelmed** by another's feelings. This happens when your internal boundary is either non-existent or damaged. **Induced feelings** can cause you to feel **crazy**: these feelings don't make sense because they are not your own.

- **Frozen Feelings from your Childhood** result from being **attacked** physically and/or verbally as a child for having and showing feelings. Feelings elicited *during child abuse* can be so overwhelming and miserable that you may have shut down emotionally and **frozen** your feelings just to survive.

♥ Experiencing little or no emotion is a position of **apparent** safety or advantage. (Example: a boy received frequent physical beatings from his father, and when he cried, his father would intensify the beating and say 'Boys don't cry! Stop that!' Then the boy would cut himself off from his feelings to avoid a worse beating).

♥ Healing from minimization, denial, and delusion requires a **breakthrough**. In the process you may **tap into** buried childhood feelings you froze a long time ago. As your feelings thaw, they will often **leak out** through your tears. You may feel **extremely vulnerable**/childlike (very different from your adult feelings), because your feelings seem **very old** when they thaw and you may resist feeling them: 'I can't feel this because if I do, I will die'.

◆ **Adult-to-child Carried Feeling Reality**

♥ As a child you **absorbed** feelings such as shame, rage, fear, and pain from the adults who *abused* you. Child abuse occurs when adults are *behaving shamelessly*, and not being accountable for their behaviors.

♥ *Feelings induced by abusive adults* remain within you into adulthood and are called 'carried feelings' because they have been **carried forward** from your childhood. Carried feelings are often experienced as **overwhelming** and out-of-control!

◆ **Signals of Feeling Realities:**

♥ Feeling **centered** = Adult Feeling Reality

♥ Feeling **crazy** = Adult Induced Feeling Reality

♥ Feeling **vulnerable** and childlike = Frozen Feelings from your Childhood

♥ Feeling **overwhelmed** and out of control = Adult-to-child Carried Feelings

VI. experiential exercises

◆ **Didactic Exercise**: Guidelines to create safety: listen to hear, be accepting and non-judgmental, no rescuing/care-taking. Honestly share your feeling with your partner, along with the thoughts/experiences preceding the feeling.

◆ **Group**: Which feelings where you able to express in your family? Whose pattern of feeling were you able to express in your family?

VII. homework

1. **Feeling Journal**: Make a list of the **emotions** you felt during the day, along with the events connected to them, and identify which feelings you were **able or unable** to experience and express. Are you still responding the way you did as a child, or have you changed your feeling responses?

2. **Feeling Response List**: Make a list of the things you **could** have been angry, scared, happy, guilty, lonely, or felt pain/shame about. In which situations were you able to **express** your feelings and in which situations did you **hold back** from expressing your feelings? Are you still responding the way you did as a child, or have you changed your feeling responses?

3. **Writing Exercise**: Choose **one** of the following words and write about how you are experiencing your feelings about whatever surfaces:

anger	fear	lack of love
attacked	frustration	loss of faith in God
betrayed	forgiveness	loss of faith in self
blame (self or others)	God	low self-esteem
brother	grief	miffed
contempt	heaviness	mother
dead dreams	hopelessness	need to be loved
deceived		no belief in healing
deprived		no belief in life
disgust		numb
dissatisfied		punish
disturbed		punishment
dread		resistance
dysfunction		sister
emotionally repressed		trapped
evil		undeserving of love
expectations		untrusting
father		withdrawal

experiencing feelings and their gifts

FEELINGS	GIFTS
ANGER	Assertiveness, energy, strength, clarity
Resentful	
Irritated	
Frustrated	
Aggravated	
Agitated	
Bitter	
Pessimistic	
Disgusted	
Furious	
Exasperated	
Enraged	
Infuriated	
FEAR	Protection, preservation, wisdom, discernment, courage, increased self-esteem
Apprehensive	
Overwhelmed	
Threatened	
Anxious	
Afraid	
Terrified	
Startled	
Nervous	
Panicky	
Worried	
Anguished	
Cautious	
Shocked	
Surprised	
Frightened	
Scared	
Jittery	
Horrified	
Troubled	
Hesitant	
Uncomfortable	
Uneasy	
Fretting	
Trapped	

PAIN	Healing, understanding, growth, wisdom, compassion, greater connection, cleansing
Sad	
Gloomy	
Distressed	
Disheartened	
Dismayed	
Hurt	
Loss	
Pity	
Disappointed	
Depressed	
Lonely	
Troubled	
Helpless	
Grieving	
Overwhelmed	
Distant	
Discouraged	
Despondent	
Withdrawn	
Apathetic	
Weary	
LOVE	Connection, surrender, acceptance, serenity, trust, contentment, peace, intimacy
Warmth	
Affectionate	
Tender	
Appreciative	
Compassionate	
Grateful	
Trusting	
Friendly	
Sensitive	
Caring	
Gentle	
Kind	
Nurtured	

JOY	Abundance, gratitude, confidence, vitality
Happy	
Elated	
Hopeful	
Exuberant	
Giddy	
Alive	
Invigorated	
Energetic	
Confident	
Delighted	
Proud	
Satisfied	
Touched	
PASSION	Appetite, energy, excitement, inspiration, life force
Zestful	
Ecstatic	
Encouraged	
Refreshed	
Stimulated	
Alive	
Exuberant	
Adventurous	
Motivated	
SHAME	Humility, containment, humanity
Embarrassed	
Humble	
Exposed	
Confused	
GUILT	Honesty, realignment, truth, values
Regretful	
Contrite	
Remorseful	
Suspicious	

carried feelings body chart

When you are unable to express your feeling reality, your unexpressed feelings will locate in a part or parts of your body and eventually evolve into physical symptoms and problems.

1. **Where in your body are you *now* noticing any particular sensations?**
2. **How do you recognize and name them? Are these familiar/unfamiliar?**
3. **What feelings are you noticing that are coming up right now?**
4. **Where in your body are you feeling them?**
5. **Circle words, draw on the figure, and write your responses on this chart.**

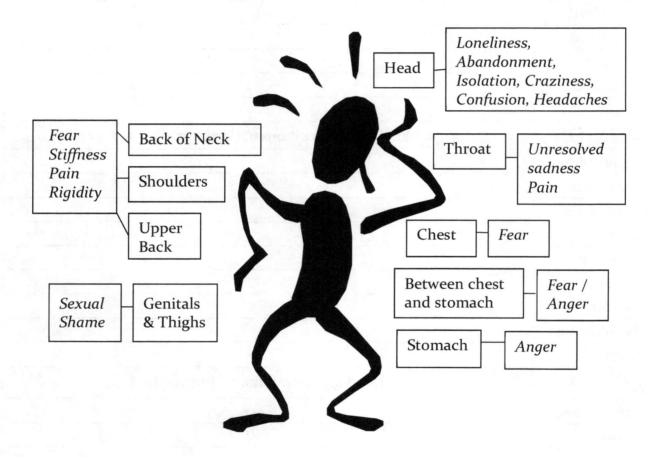

Head — *Loneliness, Abandonment, Isolation, Craziness, Confusion, Headaches*

Fear Stiffness Pain Rigidity — Back of Neck / Shoulders / Upper Back

Throat — *Unresolved sadness Pain*

Chest — *Fear*

Between chest and stomach — *Fear / Anger*

Stomach — *Anger*

Sexual Shame — Genitals & Thighs

Free-floating or undifferentiated body aches and pain are due to SHAME.

68 © 2013 Darcy S. Clarke info@LivingInAlignment.ca

feelings and defenses worksheet

Below, circle the FEELINGS that you try to deny or hide from yourself and others. Add other feelings that are not on the list.	Below, list the DEFENSES that you use to cover up or hide the respective feeling: rationalizing, analyzing, explaining, sarcasm, joking, silence, judging, justifying, threatening, attacking, apologizing, avoiding, debating, blaming, running away, generalizing, defying, arguing, denying, put-downs, demanding, minimizing, food, alcohol, sex, exercise, drugs, working, switching the subject, others:, TV	Below, describe how others might PERCEIVE you when you use defenses: arrogant, stubborn, phony, hostile, martyr, intolerant, superior, defiant, nice guy/girl, suspicious, aloof, rejecting, punishing, indifferent, others:, agreeable, threatening, stubborn, being smug, wishy-washy, distant, martyr, talking too much, people-pleasing
Angry		
Sad		
Afraid		
Hurt		
Guilty		
Lonely		
Ashamed		
Mad		
Glad		
Hopeless		
Depressed		
Helpless		
Frustrated		
Resentful		
Worried		
Nervous		
Confused		
Insecure		
Embarrassed		

close all exits!

Check some of the ways you try to escape from whatever is uncomfortable:

Leave Physically:
☐ Walk Out
☐ Exercise
☐ Fall Asleep
☐ Feel Paralyzed
☐ Get Sick
☐ Have Accidents
☐ Clean the House/Office
☐ Strike Out Physically

Leave Mentally:
☐ Dissociate
☐ Rationalize
☐ Change the Subject
☐ Intellectualize
☐ Make Mental Lists
☐ Analyze
☐ Agree to Forget About It
☐ Fight

Leave Emotionally:
☐ Get Angry
☐ Shut Down
☐ Talk Incessantly
☐ Become Ambivalent
☐ Experience Self-doubt
☐ Become Confused

Move Into a Defense Mode:
☐ Become Self-righteous
☐ Feel Criticized
☐ Become Resentful
☐ Justify
☐ Get Indignant
☐ Lie

Indulge an Addiction:
☐ Eat
☐ Shop
☐ Watch Television
☐ Act Out Sexually
☐ Relate Compulsively
☐ Work
☐ Fantasize
☐ Gamble
☐ Use Alcohol/Drugs
☐ _____
☐ _____

7. your needs and wants

I. what are your basic needs?

- ◆ Every person has basic **needs** and individual **wants**.

- ◆ **Needs** are identified as those things **you** must have to survive:

  ☐ **Physical**: food, water, air, clothing, shelter, medical/dental care, safety, physical affection, rest.

  ☐ **Emotional:** time, warmth, tenderness, caring, bonding, comfort. In relationships it manifests as interdependence: how feelings are shared, heard, and responded to.

  ☐ **Spiritual:** expression of spirituality as an individual, as a couple, as a community, with respect for differences. Beauty/aesthetic, harmony/peace, grace, inspiration, being, freedom, choice, individuality, self-empowerment, solitude, integrity, self-worth, respect, authenticity, visions/dreams.

  ☐ **Self-expression:** meaning, creativity, healing, purpose, teaching, goals, contributing, growth, mastery.

  ☐ **Celebration of life:** play, aliveness, intensity, stimulation, excitement, passion, pleasure, delight, humor, mourning, communion, ritualizing the sacred.

  ☐ **Intellectual:** values, beliefs, studies, problem-solving, stimulation, clarity, to understand/comprehend, information, awareness/consciousness, thinking, reflection, analyzing, discrimination.

  ☐ **Sexual:** expression of sexuality (or desire for sexuality) within a marriage or committed partnership, how these issues are discussed, when and where these issues will be verbalized.

  ☐ **Financial resources:** earning, saving, spending, budgeting, and investing money.

- ◆ **Wants** can be either **preferences** (things you don't have to have, but when you choose them they bring you great joy), or that which takes your life in a general direction and brings you **fulfillment** including: 'I want to be married to this person', or 'I want to be a doctor', or 'I want to develop this corporation', or 'I want to have a child'.

II. codependence and dysfunction

- ◆ It was up to your major caregivers to **meet your needs** as a child. It was also the responsibility of your major caregivers to teach you the skill base to **satisfy your needs** and wants for yourself.

- ◆ As an adult **you are responsible** to identify and address your needs/wants and ask for assistance when needed.

♦ If you have experienced **insufficient nurturing around your interconnectedness** with other people, you may experience **difficulty** accessing your needs and wants and getting them met.

♦ When this occurs, one of four scenarios is likely to occur:

☐ **You become too dependent:** you expect others to know and meet your needs for you. The person who becomes dependent often comes from a family where the caregivers met all of the child's needs and wants without **teaching** him how to meet those needs/wants himself or with the assistance of others.

☐ **You become anti-dependent:** you take the stance that you **alone** can/should meet your own needs and that no one else can/should help you. Often children who are attacked for having any needs or wants grow up to be anti-dependent. You may have learned that it is **unsafe** to ask an adult to meet any of your needs. If you were told that your needs and wants are wrong and inappropriate, you may grow up not **trusting** yourself to meet your needs/wants.

☐ **You become needless/wantless:** you are not aware of your needs or wants. Children who were **neglected** and/or abandoned by their caregivers often grow up with feelings of being needless/wantless. At a young age you may have learned to 'turn off' your needs, as you are induced to believe that you are **not important** enough to have them. You may become adept at attending to others' needs without **recognizing** your own. You feel **guilty** when someone meets one of your needs.

☐ **You confuse wants and needs:** you attempt to **meet your needs by getting what you want** (buying clothes when what you really need is physical intimacy). Children whose parents are wealthy often experience confusion about their wants and needs. Instead of getting the guidance and support they need, they are **given** something. As an adult you may often fill the need for **intimacy** and real relationships by **buying** something to fill that **void**.

♦ Wanting and needing love, acceptance, respect, intimacy, support, encouragement, physical affection, connection, understanding, friendship, appreciation, etc. are natural and **healthy desires**.

♦ A certain amount of **emotional dependence** is present in most relationships, including the healthiest ones. It is when you become **driven and controlled** by this need, or when other people become **the key to your happiness** that emotional dependence becomes a problem.

♦ Codependence stems from a lack of **self-esteem**. When you have been abandoned and neglected so often, you come to believe that **you are not good enough**, that something is wrong with you, that you don't matter, etc. These shaming beliefs foster self-hatred, and in the process you abandon yourself: needing people, yet believing that you are unlovable and that people will never be there for you.

♦ Not being **centered** in yourself and not feeling emotionally **secure** with yourself is likely to **trap** you. You may become **afraid** to terminate relationships that are dead and destructive. Too much **dependence** on another person can kill love. Relationships based on emotional insecurity and need rather than on love can become **self-destructive**. They don't work. Too much **neediness** drives people away and smothers love. It scares people away and attracts the wrong type of people. Your **real needs** don't get met and thus become greater, and so does your **despair**.

III. recovery: your interdependence with others

♦ **Interdependence** is a desirable balance wherein you acknowledge and meet your healthy, natural needs for people and love, yet you don't become overly or harmfully dependent on them.

♦ **Characteristics of interdependent relationships** (Weinhold 218)

☐ You both recognize that behavioral patterns based on fears and unhealed wounds from childhood are to be **worked through**, and agree that a focus of your relationship is overcoming and healing these core issues.

☐ You both commit to **stay with conflicts** until personal awareness and resolution occur.

☐ You both intend that relationships with self/others serve as **catalysts** of your healing and growth.

☐ You see relationships as **a discovery process**. Your intention is to discover and understand more about yourself and your partner and not try to change him/her.

☐ Instead of being naïve, you **trust yourself deeply**.

☐ As you both are **working on** all five core life skills, you can be hurt less by your partner and you will be less likely to hurt your partner. You both hold yourselves **accountable** and take individual responsibility. You **trust** that your partner will take care of him/herself and that he/she will ask for what he/she needs and wants from you and vice versa.

☐ Your partner is your **mirror** to help you see aspects of yourself that you have difficulty with or avoid seeing in yourself.

☐ You both focus on each person's **relationship with himself/herself**. Your partner agrees to cooperate and support your relationship with yourself and vice versa.

☐ You both recognize that **children** can help you become more self-aware and enable you to **deepen** your ability to love yourself and others.

☐ You both resolve conflicts with children in ways that don't unduly frustrate a child's search for **autonomy**. You both focus on getting to know them and learning from them, as opposed to trying to **control** them.

☐ You both recognize that these principles apply to **all relationships**, including student-teacher, employee-employer, friend-colleague, and nation-to-nation relationships.

☐ Others:

♦ **Qualities experienced in interdependent relationships:**

☐ closeness	☐ understanding	☐ trust	☐ relaxation
☐ connection	☐ being heard	☐ reassurance	☐ emotional freedom
☐ communication	☐ support	☐ love	☐ emotional safety
☐ consideration	☐ cooperation	☐ acceptance	☐ predictability
☐ respect	☐ appreciation	☐ affection	☐ consistency
☐ fairness	☐ admiration	☐ being liked	☐ reliability
☐ equality	☐ acknowledgement	☐ sharing intimacy	☐ stability
☐ tolerance	☐ recognition	☐ friendship	☐ vulnerability
☐ justice	☐ validation	☐ companionship	☐ compassion

Others:

♦ These experiences can come about as you learn to **love** yourself, **protect** yourself, **acknowledge** yourself, **nurture** yourself, and live in **moderation**. In the process of healing from codependence, **your life becomes transformed** as you learn to become *separate, whole,* and *autonomous*.

♦ Within interdependent relationships, you are free to be yourself. You come to realize that **you are loved for who you really are**, not for some kind of image you tried to create. In these relationships you can have and express your thoughts, feelings, and experiences.

IV. the continuum of relationships from nourishing to toxic

☐ A **very nourishing relationship** has high levels of both awareness and commitment. Both you and your partner contribute greatly to each other's healing/growth.

☐ A **mildly nourishing relationship** has lower levels of awareness or commitment in some areas, which reduces the contribution that each of you makes to the other's life.

☐ A **non-contributing relationship** occurs when the awareness level and contribution to growth and learning is sufficiently low enough that each of you makes little or no contribution to the other's personal development.

☐ A **mildly toxic relationship** occurs when there is so little awareness and commitment that each of you feels slightly diminished as a person, and your relationship interferes with your enjoyment of life.

☐ A **very toxic relationship** occurs when there is no noticeable commitment to growth. Instead there are excessive demands, hostility, and verbal and/or physical abuse that is very damaging to both of you.

8. examining your beliefs and cognitions

Reality is what we take to be true. What we take to be true is what we believe. What we believe is based upon our perceptions. What we perceive depends upon what we look for. What we look for depends upon what we think. What we think depends upon what we perceive. What we perceive determines what we believe. What we believe determines what we take to be true. What we take to be true is our reality. —Gary Zukav

I. your beliefs create codependence

◆ Your **beliefs** are the fabric of your life. Along with other **cognitions** they become the underpinnings of your thinking, whether or not you are conscious of them.

◆ Your mind is the sum total of **your conditioning**: your beliefs, thought forms, attitudes, perceptions, expectations, assumptions, judgments, and interpretations.

◆ The good news is that beliefs and cognitions can be **modified or changed** altogether.

◆ You can also develop **new** beliefs and cognitions to replace those that you have discarded.

◆ You can examine your beliefs and cognitions and determine for yourself which, if any, are **limiting you**, not serving you, or getting in the way of your recovery.

◆ Until you do that you will remain **in the dark** and be unable to understand their impact on **all** aspects of your life, be it in relationships, living up to your full potential, living authentically, finding meaning and purpose in what you do, manifesting, and experiencing fulfillment.

◆ From the perspective of this recovery model, codependence is a set of **maladaptive patterns** of dysfunctional behavior, expectations, and beliefs about yourself and others. You absorbed these codependent patterns from your experiences, but they have become hardened into the self-reinforcing concrete of **your unyielding beliefs and cognitions**.

♦ When you insist that your codependent beliefs and cognitions about yourself and your codependent interactions with others are the only reasonable and logical way to live, you become **trapped in what you expect to happen**.

♦ You are unconsciously **co-creating your codependent reality**. The first breakthrough is finally realizing that you can't go on this way. At that point you may be open to examining and **challenging your belief system**.

♦ *Your beliefs are thoughts that become set energy patterns when repeated over and over again.* Beliefs function like **lenses** that promote your seeing life from a particular point of view. They will actually **filter out** all information that could challenge or disprove them and will find only supporting evidence to validate your beliefs.

II. adopting other people's beliefs and cognitions

♦ You may be surprised to discover that what you consider to be your beliefs are in actuality **the beliefs of others** that you have adopted. The beliefs you share with others form the common bonds that develop into friendships, support groups, organizations, marriages, and business partnerships. Beliefs **divide people as well**, leading to discrimination, marginalization, divisiveness, and in extreme cases, war.

♦ Your mind receives information like a sponge. You are easily susceptible to **societal conditioning** before you develop the capacity to think for yourself. This is why your so-called 'formative' years, especially from infancy through early childhood, have so much impact on your character development.

♦ People who share the same beliefs create **an energy field** that can be quite powerful. This energy has the potential to be highly influential. Depending on how it is channeled, it can be used to **unify** as easily as to **divide**.

♦ You will want to be discerning about those with whom you associate as well as the organizations with which you affiliate, for you will tend to **take on their beliefs**. This includes all social systems—familial, religious, educational, political, corporate.

♦ Your family of origin has **a particularly powerful influence** on your life. Your individuation and differentiation are greatly impacted by your early conditioning. These factors include: (1) your earliest contact, when you were **most susceptible** to conditioning; (2) the **dependence** you had on your primary care givers to provide for your basic needs; (3) the close **proximity** and duration of time spent with the family.

♦ Developing your processing skills will help ensure that the beliefs and cognitions you hold are **truly your own** and not those that have been imposed on you by other people or institutions.

III. your indoctrination into codependence

- The socialization process can be viewed as a form of **indoctrination**. The public education system has prepared you to assimilate into **the dominant culture**. Enforcing conformity to stereotypical roles and vocational choices often has the effect of stunting your process of individuation and differentiation.

- You are expected to conform to the dominant social system. The media are a pervasive influence in perpetuating conformity. Indoctrination has become **an unconscious process** for many of us.

- Thus it is an important to develop your **awareness skills** to identify the subtle and pervasive nature of your **acculturation process**.

- Your judgments, perceptions, emotions, and body sensations bring you face to face with your beliefs. You can examine **what is actually happening** in your interactions with others to discern which beliefs and cognitions you are utilizing.

- You always get to decide which of your beliefs you want to keep, modify, or change altogether.

IV. the power of your belief system

- What you say '**I am**' to has a way of claiming your life. Before a belief becomes a belief, it is a **message** or thought form. As you focus on it by repeating it over and over again, it develops into an **energetic pattern**.

- Beliefs create powerful vortices of energy. They can become a **springboard** to your freedom as easily as they can keep you **chained** to what you don't want. When you state, '**I am an alcoholic**,' you are in effect **identifying with your condition** rather than saying 'I have alcoholism.' When you over-identify with or internalize your conditions, you proclaim that **you *are* your conditions**.

V. what you know vs. what you believe

- Believing and knowing are **not necessarily** one and the same.

- Knowing is the result of **having experienced** something directly, while believing something is not necessarily based on subjective experience. Believing can be a **purely intellectual** understanding that is logical, linear, and rational. In other words it makes sense to you.

- You may also have **beliefs that you do not actually agree with** because something was instilled in your mind at an early age. Certain of your beliefs have always been there or have become so pervasive that you are unconscious of them.

- *Your beliefs and cognitions directly impact your emotions as well as your behaviors.* Unexamined beliefs and cognitions will **always** have an impact on all aspects of your life.

- You can both believe in something and at the same time have knowledge of it. You can believe that Source energy exists, and at the same time **know** this is true based on **your subjective experiences** of a higher Power working in your life.

VI. your beliefs and interpretations

♦ Beliefs develop from how your mind interprets the events, circumstances, and conditions that surround you. Your interpretations are affected by many variables, including your current beliefs, that function as both **lenses and filters**.

♦ Your beliefs directly impact your interpretations, while your interpretations reinforce your beliefs. If your beliefs do not facilitate your own best interests, they will **help you perpetuate what you don't want**.

♦ This is why it is so **important to identify and examine your beliefs**: they hold the key to **understanding and changing the realities** you are constantly co-creating.

♦ Your mind can be a loyal servant or terrible tyrant. Yet you must not treat your mind as an enemy or something to be annihilated. **Your soul needs your mind** (and your human self) to **accomplish its mission** in life.

♦ You are deprogramming and reprogramming your mind, **not your soul. You decide** which beliefs and cognitions you want to change or replace. This model promotes developing beliefs and cognitions that facilitate **soul realization**, **soul actualization**, and **soul fulfillment**.

VII. when your beliefs and cognitions are in the way

♦ When your human self is in the driver's seat, your overall sense of wellbeing becomes jeopardized because **you are not living in the truth** of who you are.

♦ When you are internally resourced, you are in relationship with both your soul and your human self. In establishing this partnership **your human self merges with your soul**, which then helps ensure that the needs of both get met.

♦ Your soul will inform your human self when **limiting beliefs and cognitions** are getting in the way. Some of the most common signs of **having lost your way** include:

☐ feeling stuck

☐ repeating unwanted dysfunctional behavioral patterns such as addictions and self-deprecation

☐ judging yourself and/or others

☐ comparing yourself to other people or relating to them from a one-up or one-down position

☐ feeling out of balance, over-extended, resentful, or on the verge of burnout

☐ experiencing unhappiness or angst

☐ feeling disconnected from yourself and your relationships

☐ not knowing what your needs are

☐ exhibiting poor health

☐ being inauthentic

☐ feeling that your heart is closed

- ☐ knowing somehow that your life has taken a wrong turn
- ☐ feeling unfulfilled
- ☐ reacting versus responding to what is happening in your life
- ☐ being highly defended
- ☐ feeling anxiety-ridden
- ☐ attempting to control others
- ☐ experiencing a lack of spontaneity
- ☐ being cynical

♦ These are indications that your beliefs and cognitions are **sabotaging** your life. You need to look inward to identify and examine the particulars of how your human self is getting in your way.

♦ Beliefs and cognitions do not get modified or change on their own accord. It takes a **conscious effort** on your part. This does not translate to endless processing, but it will demand **discipline**, **determination**, **attentiveness**, and **courage**.

VIII. skills to work with your beliefs and cognitions

♦ This recovery model teaches life skills that are vital to **deprogramming** and **reprogramming** your beliefs and cognitions. These include:

- ☐ re-parenting yourself
- ☐ becoming your own best friend/ally
- ☐ challenging your beliefs
- ☐ letting go and letting God
- ☐ developing an attitude of gratitude
- ☐ recognizing that you always have choices
- ☐ becoming solution-oriented
- ☐ reframing your thoughts
- ☐ being fully aware of each day's opportunities
- ☐ developing mindfulness skills
- ☐ working with energy

♦ Focusing on and **clarifying your intentions** is one of the most effective ways to access your soul, creating **a powerful energy vortex** of laser beam-like precision.

♦ Your intentions help your human self bypass the trappings of your limiting beliefs and cognitions in order to access directly what is most important.

♦ Your intentions will help your human self get out of its limiting 'story' by **expanding** your awareness: looking for the **opportunities** in your life and tuning into 'what wants to happen' or **what your heart is longing to experience**.

♦ You can review your 'story' and **examine all your options** from the perspective of expanded consciousness. Focusing on your intentions in this way will help to keep you **empowered**.

IX. working directly with your beliefs and cognitions

♦ Become aware of your beliefs and cognitions in the context of your **moment-to-moment** experiencing. This requires awareness, which requires **being present**.

♦ Do not become **hypervigilant**, getting caught up in the thought of being present rather than the experience.

♦ Become conscious of being present by learning to pay attention to **what is happening inside** as well as outside yourself.

♦ When you recognize that you have **tripped up** on your unconscious belief system, you can then channel the energy necessary to **modify, change, or replace** your limiting belief or cognition.

♦ Challenge your thinking by counteracting your prejudice with **the larger picture** that is more congruent with your truth.

♦ If your mind is saying that being present is too much work, the truth is that it requires even **more time, energy, and work** when you are **not** present in your life. Why?

♦ Because the **less present** you are, the more you are **missing out** on what is actually happening in your moment-to-moment experiencing.

♦ When you become **more present**:

☐ you have **more time** to linger in the enjoyable moments.

☐ you can identify and **integrate** all the insights, gifts, and lessons being offered.

☐ you can remain **empowered** in all your relationships.

☐ you can make conscious and well-informed **choices and decisions**.

☐ you can keep your **energy field** clear.

☐ you can identify and meet **your human and soul needs** more effectively.

☐ you are **nourished** energetically.

☐ you can experience more **joy, happiness, and fulfillment**.

♦ Your ability to be present will not be perfect, but you can **improve with practice**.

X. conclusion

♦ This process is intended to **affirm, inspire, excite, and motivate** you. It is a wakeup call to help you realize that **the world within is just as real** as the world without (if not more so), and that an incredible journey awaits you, one of awakening to the magnificence of who you are while appreciating the wonders that surround you.

♦ You are invited to open your mind and entertain these constructs from the perspective of 'What if it is true?'. ***You are integrating your own truth***, accessed from the personal insights, gifts, and lessons learned from your subjective experiences.

♦ You are not expected to replace one set of beliefs with another, but rather to **test out** this approach and allow **your own experiences** to determine the validity, viability, and reliability of what you perceive. You will be able to make a conscious and well-informed decision about which constructs to integrate into your own truth.

♦ Your human self will want your beliefs and cognitions to be as congruent as possible with the whole truth of who you are. When shifts (permanent changes) take place in your internal reality (energetically, mentally, emotionally, physically, and behaviorally), they will be reflected in all aspects of your external reality. This model is intended to assist you to access your own truth concerning every aspect of your life and help you develop a skill base so that you can embody this truth.

♦ This is a life-long process of deepening in relationship to your human self and your soul, which in turn facilitates deepening in all your relationships, including the one you have with life itself. You will become more conscious of this process as well as experience its benefits every step of the way.

Man often becomes what he believes himself to be. If I keep on saying to myself that I cannot do a certain thing, it is possible that I may end by really becoming incapable of doing it. On the contrary, if I have the belief that I can do it, I shall surely acquire the capacity to do it, even if I may not have it at the beginning. —Mahatma Gandhi

XI. activities to explore your beliefs and cognitions

1. Do a stream-of-consciousness writing on "When I think about the impact of the past on my personality, what surfaces is..."

2. On a blank sheet of paper, write the statement "impact of the past" in the center of the paper, then jot down all the words and phrases that come to mind as you are contemplating that statement.

3. Do a stream-of-consciousness writing on "When I think about beliefs having a direct impact on co-creating my life, what surfaces is..."

4. List the beliefs you have about yourself, Source energy, other people, and life in general.

5. Make a list of the things (attributes, characteristics, features, traits) that you do not like about yourself. State the reasons.

6. Think about the last time you had a different opinion, belief, or perception from someone else... How did you interact with that person? What did you say to yourself?

7. What is your typical response to people attempting to impose their beliefs, perceptions, and opinions on you?

8. If you perceive that other people's beliefs, opinions, or perceptions may be potentially harmful, what do you say and/or do?

9. Write about a belief, perception, or attitude that you have since modified or changed. What are your experiences like? How did it change you or your life?

10. Do a stream-of-consciousness writing on "When I think about having my own beliefs, thoughts, perceptions, opinions, what surfaces is..."

Believe nothing just because a so-called wise person said it.
Believe nothing just because a belief is generally held.
Believe nothing just because it is said in ancient books.
Believe nothing just because it is said to be of divine origin.
Believe nothing just because someone else believes it.
Believe only what you yourself test and judge to be true.
—The Buddha [paraphrased]

defense mechanisms worksheet

A. Circle ALL of the following conditions you have been told you have or *think* you have:

1) Alcoholism, Drug Addiction, Sex Addiction, Process Addictions, Bipolar, Depression, Anti-social, Obsessive Compulsive Disorder, Eating Disorder.

2) Others:_____

B. Describe how you *feel* about your condition(s):

_____

_____

_____

_____

C. Have you *accepted* your condition(s)? Yes or No? Please explain:

_____

_____

D. What is *preventing* you from accepting your condition(s)? Please explain:

_____

_____

_____

E. Referring to the list below, identify which *defense mechanisms* you use to hide from your feelings, your condition(s), or use to justify your behavior(s):

☐ alcohol	☐ defying	☐ joking	☐ sex
☐ analyzing	☐ demanding	☐ judging	☐ silence
☐ apologizing	☐ denying	☐ justifying	☐ threatening
☐ arguing	☐ drugs	☐ minimizing	☐ TV
☐ attacking	☐ exercise	☐ put-downs	☐ working
☐ avoiding	☐ explaining	☐ rationalizing	☐ switching the subject
☐ blaming	☐ food	☐ running away	
☐ debating	☐ generalizing	☐ sarcasm	☐ others:

distorted thinking

- ☐ **All-or-nothing thinking:** You look at things in absolute, black-and-white categories.

- ☐ **Overgeneralization:** You view a negative event as a never-ending pattern of defeat.

- ☐ **Mental filter:** You dwell on the negatives and ignore the positives.

- ☐ **Discounting the positives:** You insist that your accomplishments or positive qualities don't count.

- ☐ **Jumping to conclusions:** You conclude things are bad without any definite evidence.

- ☐ **Mind reading:** You assume people are reacting negatively to you.

- ☐ **Catastrophizing:** You predict that things will turn out badly.

- ☐ **Magnification or minimization:** You blow things way out of proportion or you shrink their importance.

- ☐ **Emotional reasoning:** You reason from how you feel: 'I feel like an idiot, so I must be one.'

- ☐ **'Should' statements:** You criticize yourself or other people with 'shoulds', 'should nots', 'musts', 'oughts', and 'have-tos.'

- ☐ **Labeling:** Instead of saying, 'I made a mistake', you tell yourself, '**I AM** a mistake'.

- ☐ **Blame:** You blame yourself for something you weren't entirely responsible for, or you blame other people and overlook ways that you contributed to a problem.

- ☐ **Being right:** You are continually on trial to prove that your opinions and actions are correct. Being wrong is unthinkable.

- ☐ **Control Fallacies:** You tell yourself that you are helpless and a victim of fate. You feel responsible for the pain and happiness of everyone around you.

- ☐ **Fallacy of Change:** You expect that other people will change to suit you if you just pressure or cajole them enough. You need to change people because your hopes for happiness seem to depend entirely on them.

- ☐ **Fallacy of Fairness:** You are resentful because you think you know what's fair and other people won't agree with you.

- ☐ **Filtering:** You take the negative details and magnify them while filtering out all positive aspects of a situation.

- ☐ **Global labeling:** You generalize one or two qualities into a negative global judgment.

- ☐ **Heaven's reward fallacy:** You expect all your sacrifice and self-denial to pay off, as if there was someone keeping score. You feel bitter when the reward doesn't come.

- ☐ **Personalization:** You think that everything people do or say is some kind of reaction to you. You also compare yourself to others, trying to determine who's smarter, better, looking, etc.

distorted thinking log

*See **previous page** for examples of cognitive distortions.*

Circumstance, Experience, or Event	Cognitive Distortions	Self-affirming Statement
Example: Illness (of any kind)	*'God is punishing me'* is **JUMPING TO CONCLUSIONS.**	*Illness is not punishment. It can offer me insight and compassion.*

personal notes:

9. living in moderation

I. extreme patterns of living

♦ Not knowing **how to be moderate** is possibly the pattern of codependence most visible to other people. For anyone in a codependent relationship, trying to deal with a partner who cannot contain him/herself and is always **acting in one extreme** is very difficult.

☐ When you have difficulty experiencing and expressing your reality moderately, you do not appear to understand **what moderation is**.

☐ You believe that a moderate response to a situation isn't enough: **only too much is enough.** All four aspects of your reality (physical, thinking, feeling, behaviors) manifest extreme patterns.

☐ Moderation is essentially about **your self-containment** and is related to both your boundary and reality issues. When you erect a **wall** to contain yourself, you tend to shut down and wall others out. In this process you '**lose control of being in control**' of yourself and others. When you have **no boundaries** with which to contain yourself, you will do whatever you want to do, disregarding your impact on others.

♦ You may **care for your body in the extreme**: you may dress immoderately to hide your body, wearing baggy/bland clothes (especially likely if you have been sexually abused). The other extreme is dressing flamboyantly in skimpy, tight, clinging clothes, clearly revealing your body to everyone. Physical extremes may also involve how fat or thin you become.

Your lack of containment may also manifest in **extreme habits of self-care or no habits at all**: being either compulsively neat or sloppy in your personal grooming.

♦ **In the cognitive realm**, containment issues can manifest in your propensity for

☐ black-and-white thinking.

☐ thinking in terms of right/wrong, good/bad.

☐ seeing few gray areas.

☐ jumping to conclusions.

☐ making assumptions.

☐ catastrophizing.

☐ having difficulty in seeing options in your life and/or believing that there is only one right answer.

♦ **In relationships**, your lack of containment can manifest as believing that 'If you don't agree with me completely, you are totally against me.'

♦ **Solutions to problems are extreme**. If you have containment issues and something about you is bothering another person, your solution could be to think that you should never see that person again to avoid offending them.

♦ **In the feeling realm**, you may have difficulty experiencing/expressing your feelings moderately if you have containment issues: either you feel little or no emotions or you have explosive and/or agonizing feelings: you are either totally happy or absolutely miserable.

♦ **Extreme behaviors:** your codependent pattern may include trusting everyone or no one at all or allowing anyone to touch you or no one to touch you. Codependent parents may discipline their children severely or not at all. They may be totally overinvolved or totally detached.

II. origins of extreme patterns

♦ **Operating in extremes** comes from at least four types of experience:

☐ **Observing and reacting to the behavior of caregivers** who operate in extremes. When children observe their caregivers being immoderate in matters of dress, in their attitude towards their bodies, in the way they think and solve problems, in the expression of their feelings and/or in the behavior they model, they will **question** them, **adopt** them as their own, or **react** to the caregiver.

For example, if you didn't like what mom and dad did, **you may do exactly the opposite**, but because what you are reacting against is extreme, your 'solution' is also extreme. The opposite of dysfunctional behavior is more dysfunctional behavior, and **that is not recovery**. Functional behavior is somewhere near **the middle** between the two extremes.

☐ The experience of **'not being heard'** or **'feeling invisible' in your family of origin**. As a child in a dysfunctional family, your dependence needs may have been **ignored** unless you behaved in an extreme manner **to get attention**. Only then would your caregivers respond to your needs. As an adult you may express yourself in **exaggerated** ways, thinking that by doing so you will be heard and noticed.

☐ If your caregivers failed to **set limits** or insisted that you be a **good or perfect** child, you may be '**in control of being out of control**' or **very controlled** and **controlling** of others.

☐ Focusing on meeting your human needs/wants while **ignoring** your soul's reality can create a **false** sense of yourself, leading to **extreme** behaviors. As you struggle with feeling **empty, lost, numb,** or **entitled,** you substitute **possessions, escapism,** intense or conflicted **relationships,** obsessive **risk-taking, compulsions,** or multiple **substance/process addictions.**

88 © 2013 Darcy S. Clarke info@LivingInAlignment.ca

learning to live in moderation

Your personal patterns may include **extreme** ways of thinking, feeling, and behaving. In the left column, **circle** the words that describe how you experience each of these codependent patterns. In the right column, **describe** how you intend to **modify or replace** your old patterns to begin **living in moderation** with yourself and others.

Extreme Patterns	Experiencing Freedom to Be
My self-esteem: disempowered, shamed, entitled, better than others, acquisition focused	I value all of who I am from within myself.
My body: ignored, endangered, hypochondriac, hidden, flaunted, obsessed about	I honor and care appropriately for my body to improve my physical health.
My thinking: confused, rigid, fear-filled, catastrophizing, blaming, controlling	I focus on realistic, truthful thinking with my internal boundary.
My feelings: absent, shut down, stuffed, emotional rollercoaster, crisis mode, blaming, controlling	I value, express, and learn from my true adult feelings and am emotionally present with myself and others.
My personal reality: denied, confusing, secretive	I know and share my experience of reality appropriately.
My 'child' reality: suppressed, denied, minimized, or obsessed about	As a functional adult I become my own loving parent, healing my wounded inner child by affirming, nurturing, and limit setting.

Extreme Patterns	Experiencing Freedom to Be
My needs/wants: unrecognized, denied, unmet, met by others	I understand and take care of both my human needs/ wants and my soul needs; I am willing to ask for help.
My decisions: reactive to others' wants, needs, feelings, priorities, opinions	I trust my perceptions, feelings, and decision-making process.
My boundaries: walls, damaged, nonexistent: I am paranoid/ invulnerable or naïve/unprotected.	I create flexible, functional boundaries, trust others appropriately, and know when to set limits and when to share intimacy.
My behavior: rigid, stereotyped, unpredictable, disorganized, quirky	I am aware of my behavior and freely responsive to life.
My identity: shame-based masks, super-achiever, under-achiever	I accept my humanness and generate my sense of identity internally.
My relationships: toxic, codependent, anti-dependent, dependent, addicted, detached, enmeshed	I am not attracted to codependence and am seeking/developing interdependent relationships.
My control issues: out-of-control, over-controlled, controlling, fixing others	I experience appropriate spontaneity and freedom to be.

V. role play exercise

♦ Ask for a volunteer who feels he/she has **containment challenges**. Ask the volunteer to choose a recent situation (outside this setting) that left him/her feeling uncomfortable. Have him/her select peers to play the role of the other characters. Now role-play the situation from both extremes. Process it with the group. Next, have the person role play the situation from the moderate/contained perspective and ask him/her to share his/her experience—what was it like? Difficult? If there is adequate time, ask peers to come up and role-play the situation, demonstrating how they might handle the situation by using appropriate containment. Point out that there is no right and wrong way. Each person's reality and truth will call for unique responses appropriate to that person.

personal notes:

10. developing your awareness

This psychospiritual recovery model embraces the perspective that the evolution of consciousness (individually and collectively) is the primary task of the human race (and all life forms). —Darcy S. Clarke

The truth is that our finest moments are most likely to occur when we are feeling deeply uncomfortable, unhappy, or unfulfilled. For it is only in such moments, propelled by our discomfort, that we are likely to step out of our ruts and start searching for different ways or truer answers. —M. Scott Peck

> *One new perception, one fresh thought, one act of surrender,*
> *one change of heart, one leap of faith, can change your life forever.*
> —Robert Holden from the book, ***Shift Happens!***

I. being present in your life

♦ Awareness is a quality of **your natural 'state of being.'** In this context, however, your 'state of being' is distinguished from your 'doing.'

♦ Awareness is the result of **being present in your life**. It is a tuning-in to the 'here-and-now' of what is happening in your moment-to-moment experiencing. You experience awareness on a continuum. Indeed, many factors (energy levels, ability to focus, receptivity, anxiety, worry, insecurity, perceptions, conditioning, etc.) contribute to increasing or decreasing your awareness from moment to moment.

♦ Awareness allows you to stay **grounded** in the seen and unseen worlds by assisting your human self to identify your responsibilities, make well-informed choices and decisions, follow your intuition, and keep in the forefront the needs of both your human self and your soul.

II. focusing your intentions

◆ Your **intentions** direct your awareness. You want to develop the habit of being present to your intentions in all of your interactions, including the ones you have with yourself. Clarity on your intentions allows you to co-create what you desire to manifest.

◆ To focus your intentions, ask yourself some of the following questions:

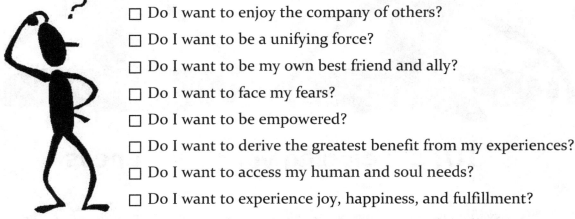

☐ Do I want to enjoy the company of others?

☐ Do I want to be a unifying force?

☐ Do I want to be my own best friend and ally?

☐ Do I want to face my fears?

☐ Do I want to be empowered?

☐ Do I want to derive the greatest benefit from my experiences?

☐ Do I want to access my human and soul needs?

☐ Do I want to experience joy, happiness, and fulfillment?

◆ Intentions help **focus** your mind in a particular way. You can then determine whether they are beneficial or detrimental. The more you focus on some aspect of your reality, the more aware you become. *Reality is defined as what is happening in the framework of your cognitions, emotions, body sensations, intuition, and circumstances.*

◆ Your **degree** of awareness has a direct impact on your ability to change your reality. When you become aware of judging someone, resolve instead to be a unifying presence. Open your heart and notice that the energy exchange becomes qualitatively different.

◆ *Coupling intention with your attention is what **deepens** your awareness.* There you discover the insights, gifts, and lessons of your moment-to-moment experiencing. Their integration will allow you to **modify** your cognitions, which will then change your external reality.

◆ If you choose awareness as a guiding practice, your life will take on a deeper sense of **meaning and purpose**. Increased awareness gives you access to 'the bigger picture' as well as to your soul mission.

III. consciously living your life

◆ You are intended to have **conscious** living experiences. *You can become increasingly aware of being conscious in all your experiences.*

◆ *Everything you do is of **significance**,* which is why you want to stay fully present in your life. Developing awareness is the lifelong practice of becoming increasingly more present.

◆ Greater awareness, both internally and externally, will help you connect the dots in whatever you do. Being aware will shine a light on how **you are co-creating your reality** on a moment-to-moment basis.

 © 2013 Darcy S. Clarke info@LivingInAlignment.ca

- You develop awareness by *staying present in your experiencing and utilizing the five senses (sight, hearing, touch, smell, and taste) as well as your* **intuition**, which is the sixth or 'soul' sense.

- The more you become aware, the more you see, feel, hear, taste, smell, and intuit. If any of your senses become impaired, the other ones will **compensate** by becoming more proficient at what they do.

- The practice of awareness is about '**being with**' and '**tuning into**' your experiences. Being aware helps you experience all aspects of your reality more fully. Greater awareness heightens your knowledge of how you want to live your life, as well as increasing your willingness to take responsibility for everything that happens.

IV. developing mindfulness

- Along with using your physical senses, **mindfulness practices** are some of the most effective ways to develop your awareness.

- Utilizing these skills will facilitate your **becoming more present** in general as well as more aware of what you are actually experiencing.

- You are training your mind to become aware, **not your soul**. These mindfulness practices have been proven to produce positive results. Here's what to do:

  - ♥ **Stay present in the here-and-now.** *Developing presence* trains your mind to slow down and encourages your human self and your soul to merge.

  - ♥ **Stay in tune with your breath.** *Breathing* brings oxygen to your physical body, focuses your mind, and fosters co-creating your life experiences.

  - ♥ **Accept what is.** *Accepting* assists your mind to stay present with what is happening rather than trying to resist it, helps you own all aspects of your reality, and allows others to have theirs.

  - ♥ **Try your best to be nonjudgmental.** *Being nonjudgmental* prevents your human self from relating to others from a one-up or one-down position, and also helps you accept your imperfections and derive greater benefit from your experiences.

  - ♥ **Remain open-hearted.** *Maintaining an open heart* nurtures your human self, increases self-esteem, and raises your energy frequency.

  - ♥ **Let go of any attachment to outcomes.** *Being unattached* assists your mind to embrace change, deepens your understanding of life cycles, and helps you remain grounded.

V. deepening your awareness

- It is your birthright to **live your life consciously.** Your awareness will increase exponentially as you become more aligned with your soul. Remember that *it is your mind that has to yield to and merge with your soul*, not the other way around.

- You can develop your awareness to become **increasingly more conscious** of your moment-to-moment experiencing. Awareness is the qualitative experience of being conscious. This is how you learn and evolve.

- With **practice** your ability to be aware will improve.

♦ You develop awareness by **becoming present**. Initially you may focus on one particular aspect of your current reality, and as you become more adept you can heighten your awareness to focus on many aspects of that reality simultaneously.

♦ The more conscious you become, the greater **access** you have to all the insights, gifts, and lessons that are always being offered. They are intended to assist you to deepen your understanding of the seen and unseen worlds. This will require staying grounded in both and taking full responsibility for your life.

♦ Living up to your full potential is about accomplishing your **soul mission**. More will always be revealed as you move forward.

♦ Deepening your awareness will facilitate accessing your **Truth** and illuminate the answers to all your questions.

♦ The voice of your **conscience** is your soul's knowing. Have you ever wondered about the conflicts going on in your mind? They may be the result of your mind bumping up against the limitations of its own conditioning or going against the best interests of your soul. Self-awareness is the key to resolving these conflicts and accessing your soul's wisdom.

VI. tuning into your direct experience of your soul

♦ Although intellectual understanding is important and necessary, **your direct experience makes an indelible impression** on your mind, and allows your human self to **merge** with your soul. Your experiences and what you obtain from them become your knowing, and your knowing cannot be denied.

♦ Having an experience and **being aware** of having that experience are not the same; the former is often limited to going through the motions, while the latter means **tuning into** the details of the 'here-and-now.'

♦ Awareness will assist you to derive the most **benefit** from your experiences by helping you identify what is being offered.

VII. changing your conditioning

♦ Awareness serves as a conduit for **deepening** your experiences of reality. The more fully you experience what is occurring internally as well as externally, the greater your understanding. Understanding leads to knowing, and knowing is Truth revealed!

♦ With practice you can develop your awareness to laser beam-like precision. Your awareness informs your perceptions, which in turn directly influence your **conditioning**: the beliefs and cognitions with which your mind identifies.

♦ It is the perspective of this model that the rightful position of your human self is to be **the agent/artist of your soul**. As such, the process of living in alignment with your soul focuses on **reprogramming your mind** to listen to and follow its promptings. In this light your human self is intended to serve as the 'vehicle,' or hands and feet of your soul. This partnership cannot be forced; instead, it must be developed.

♦ The educational system has taught you to rely on your **intellect** to direct your life. When you depend primarily on logical, linear, and rational ways of thinking,

becoming internally resourced is not an easy task. The more **cerebral** (identified with your mind as the locus of control) you become, the more difficult it will be to experience living in alignment with your soul. This is also true when you are **externally resourced**.

♦ Reprogramming your mind to be in service of your soul translates to **the 'death' of the ego** for many people. Your ego is the part of your mind that thinks it is a separate entity that has to **maintain control** of your human self.

♦ Soul realization is acknowledging that at your core you are a **unique aspect** of Source energy, and that you are both separate and one at the same time.

♦ It is important to **normalize** any **resistance** your mind may have about becoming internally resourced. It is a 'state of being' or something *you experience*. Intellectualizing is a step removed from experiencing.

VIII. avoiding awareness

♦ One of the reasons you may have not developed your awareness is that when you experience anything less than being nurtured, your human self instinctively gets triggered and goes into **survival mode**. When this occurs you erect mental and emotional **barriers** that involve anger, denial, avoidance, etc. These are just some of the coping strategies you may use to deal with what you perceive as threats to your wellbeing.

♦ As a result, you are always living in a fight-or-flight mode and/or **dissociating** from stressful experiences. You are not very present in such circumstances, and thus become **less aware** of the details of your experiences. This translates to missing out on a lot of what is being offered.

♦ **All of your experiences** *have the 'inherent potential' of serving your best interests.* This includes not only enjoyable experiences, but also those you deem to be **unpleasant**. You may close down when you get triggered. This is a maladaptive coping strategy to prevent further assault. When this happens your brain goes into a startled or 'freeze' response, which keeps you functioning in the sympathetic fight-or-flight mode, and you become **stuck** in your 'story' (the drama of what you are experiencing).

♦ If, however, you embrace the idea that **all of your experiences are serving you**, while you also work on establishing and maintaining healthy boundaries, allowing others to have their realities, identifying and getting your human and soul needs met, living in moderation, developing self-esteem, and learning to become more assertive, you will be better prepared to deal effectively with any eventuality.

♦ Identifying and working through your unresolved **trauma-related issues** will reduce triggering episodes and help you be less defensive. The more internally resourced you become, the safer your human self will feel being in the world.

♦ Perhaps you simply have not learned a process of how to become more aware. As you recognize the benefits of becoming more aware or living consciously, you become more **inspired and motivated** to develop awareness skills. One of the most important benefits of becoming more aware is that it facilitates self-empowerment.

◆ Perhaps you have not wanted to take full responsibility for your life before now. This could be because you receive a lot of **secondary benefits** from being stuck in 'victim mode'. It could also be that the primary support people in your life have been **enabling** and/or **colluding** with you (often inadvertently) to stay stuck. As long as you are not taking full responsibility for your life, you become increasingly **less empowered**.

◆ The **good news** is that in moments of insight, your human self can decide to take responsibility for your life; you can then access your soul's **guidance** on how to reclaim your life and your power.

IX. practicing awareness

◆ This model offers a language and context to prepare you to **experience your life with greater awareness**. Becoming aware will increase with practice.

◆ Disciplining your mind to focus is an integral part of this ongoing process. You develop this capacity by **focusing on the task** at hand. It doesn't matter what the task is; you must assign all tasks equal importance and approach them with thoughtfulness and attention.

◆ Your mind will tend to **wander** here, there, and everywhere. This is to be expected until your mind develops the capacity to direct its attention.

◆ **Normalizing** the wanderings of your mind will foster an acceptance of what is. Avoid judging, blaming, shaming, or getting mad at yourself for this behavior.

◆ Instead, use the fact that your mind is wandering as a cue to **come back and focus** on the task. With practice you will become better at focusing. Becoming aware requires focusing on the 'here-and-now,' on the 'what-and-how' of your experiencing. Be careful not to allow anything to become a **distraction**. It is your job to keep your mind on track.

X. awareness facilitates transformation

◆ The more aware you become of the workings of your soul, the more you will **want to experience** living in alignment with your soul.

◆ When your soul is in the driver's seat, you are never going be steered in the wrong direction. Your soul always has **your best interests** at heart (caring for both your human and soul needs).

◆ As your awareness increases, so too will **your curiosity** about the workings of your soul. In conducting retrospective overviews of your life, you will come to know that everything has a way of working itself out, especially if you are able to **identify and receive** the insights, gifts, and lessons that are being offered. If you are walking around with blinders on or just going through the motions, you will miss out on a lot of things.

◆ Being aware is a requisite of living in alignment with your soul. It is an ongoing practice that requires training your mind to **work in partnership** with your soul.

◆ Awareness is a skill that can be developed, a practice that is intended to **illuminate** your life.

◆ Instead of compartmentalizing, disassociating, avoiding, ignoring, minimizing, or completely rejecting aspects of yourself and/or your realities, you can develop awareness skills that will help you become **more accepting** of your moment-to-moment experiencing.

◆ Learning to **linger in these moments** is very important, for in doing so you gain the ability to identify, receive, and integrate what is being offered to you.

◆ The more you become aware, the more you are conscious of the **choices and opportunities** that are always before you. With increased awareness you will come to know the benefits of living in alignment with your soul in the context of your daily life. Likewise, with greater awareness you will also have a better sense of when you are **off track**, and 'get it' sooner rather than later.

◆ Awareness facilitates and is **a crucial component of any transformative process**. When awareness is coupled with an **intention** to experience greater union with yourself and all life forms, your journey of awakening becomes accelerated.

◆ In this process more and more shall be revealed about both the seen and unseen worlds. Developing your awareness leads to **soul realization**, which leads to **soul actualization** and culminates in **soul fulfillment**, or completing your **soul mission**.

◆ All of your experiences and circumstances in life have the '**inherent potential**' of serving your best interests, but unless you **tune into** the specifics of what is happening in your life, you will not gain any insights. Tuning in requires that you be present, and presence requires awareness.

◆ The following sequence depicts how awareness directly impacts co-creating your realities and **facilitates transformation**.

1. As you plug into the *hypothesis* that every experience is serving your best interests,

2. coupled with the *intention* to open your mind to the specifics of how this is so,

3. along with your *presence*

4. and your *focus* (tuning into what is),

5. you gain *access* to the insights, gifts, and lessons being offered.

6. Your task is to *integrate* them into your life.

7. Doing so *deepens* your understanding,

8. which *transforms* some aspect of your life,

9. which in turn *increases* your awareness even more.

XI. awareness vs. being externally resourced

♦ You miss out on so much that is happening in your life when you are primarily **externally resourced**. You are ruled by outside influences, living in fear, and stuck in survival mode:

☐ Your awareness is focused on taking care of your **basic needs** (food, clothing, shelter, financial stability, medical care).

☐ You are preoccupied with **a lack of resources**, thinking that you cannot trust people, that you have to keep your defenses up, that life is a struggle and then you die, that you are a sinner, that your life is about repenting, and that your higher Power is a judging, menacing, punishing force.

☐ You become **obsessed** with experiencing your life from a **dualistic** perspective: good/bad, right/wrong, positive/negative.

♦ Attending to your survival needs is absolutely necessary in order to survive. But is just surviving enough? You may acknowledge that living in a fear-based reality is **no longer an option**.

♦ You want **to thrive** instead of just surviving. From the perspective of living in alignment with your soul, thriving involves experiencing **soul realization, soul actualization**, and **soul fulfillment**: in other words, completing your **soul mission**.

XII. you have choices about how to live

♦ This recovery model asserts that **you can choose** how you want to live your life.

♦ The old paradigm of deepening awareness of your soul was about **self-sacrificing** to the point of neglecting your human needs, living in deprivation or poverty mode, associating hardship and suffering with virtue, and staying in adversarial, unsupportive, or otherwise un-nurturing conditions and/or relationships.

♦ *You can take responsibility to claim your life and **choose how you want to evolve**.*

♦ The new paradigm of becoming internally resourced is about **evolving through joy, happiness, and fulfillment**.

♦ Because these states of being increase your **energy frequency**, you will need to increase your capacity to live in these states, developing your ability to **discern** which cognitions and behaviors are **sabotaging** or preventing you from experiencing them.

♦ You will need to keep your **intention focused** on joy, happiness, and fulfillment in order to attract these states of being.

♦ As you are meeting the needs of your human self, you also need to focus on discerning and meeting **the needs of your soul**.

XIII. practicing mindful meditation

♦ Mindfulness is the practice of bringing **awareness** and **acceptance** to your moment-to-moment experience.

♦ Much of your stress comes from worrying about the future, dwelling on the past, and/or through your lack of **acceptance** of what is happening in the here and now (physical pain, emotional discomfort, life transitions, tragedy, abandonment, relationship discord, etc.).

♦ By cultivating awareness and acceptance, you can develop calmness, resiliency, and peacefulness that with practice becomes **integrated** into your daily life.

♦ There are many meditation **methods** available. Try a variety and then choose one that appeals to you.

♦ Meditation can be done by **sitting** or reclining in a comfortable position. It may involve choosing a focal point, such as the sensation of breath or other sensations or sounds. When your attention wanders, continually return it back to the focal point. Another technique involves letting your awareness float freely with no defined focal point.

♦ **Walking** mediation is another way to develop mindfulness. It involves maintaining a focus while walking: perhaps on the sensations of both feet or perhaps by coordinating your steps with the natural rhythm of your breath.

♦ Another technique involves directing your attention into the present moment by **focusing** on whatever activity is at hand (If you're listening, listen! If you're reading, read! If your washing dishes, wash the dishes!). Limit your activity to one thing at a time. ***Don't multitask!***

XIV. benefits of mindfulness and meditation

♦ Meditation is one of the most effective tools for **stress reduction**. Research findings have shown that mindfulness and various forms of meditation can contribute directly to physical, psychological, and lifestyle benefits:

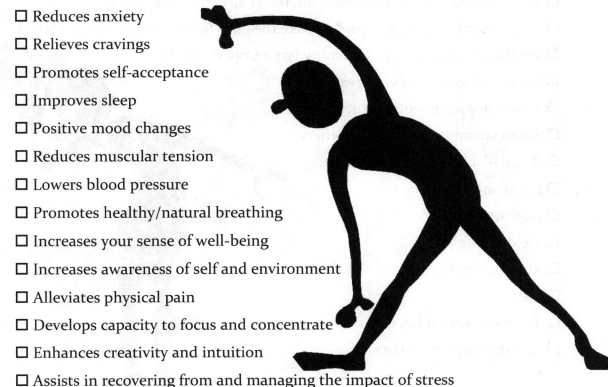

☐ Reduces anxiety

☐ Relieves cravings

☐ Promotes self-acceptance

☐ Improves sleep

☐ Positive mood changes

☐ Reduces muscular tension

☐ Lowers blood pressure

☐ Promotes healthy/natural breathing

☐ Increases your sense of well-being

☐ Increases awareness of self and environment

☐ Alleviates physical pain

☐ Develops capacity to focus and concentrate

☐ Enhances creativity and intuition

☐ Assists in recovering from and managing the impact of stress

XV. practices to develop your 'observer self'

♦ As a human being you need **meaning**. Without it you suffer from boredom, depression, hopelessness, and despair. Asked in earnest, existential questions such as 'What is the purpose of human life?', 'Who am I?', 'Who is the real me?', 'What is my life's work?' open the door to your soul.

♦ Profound despair and dull resignation are **symptoms of failing** in the search for meaning.

♦ Use of substances and process addictions may be attempts to suppress despair and to **substitute heightened sensation for meaning**.

♦ At the heart of psychopathology lies a **fundamental confusion** between the self as object and the self as direct awareness. Feelings, thoughts, impulses, images, and sensations are the contents of your consciousness. You witness them, you are aware of them, but **they are not *ALL* of who you are**.

♦ Some **practices** for developing your 'observer self':

☐ Slow down.

☐ Make time to hang out with yourself.

☐ Imagine doing less.

☐ Practice patience.

☐ Quiet your mind.

☐ Unplug your energy from the past.

☐ Tune into your body sensations and the environment around you.

☐ Avoid futurizing (if you want to make the gods laugh, tell them your plans!).

☐ Remind yourself of your humanity (your imperfection).

☐ Accept all aspects of your reality.

☐ Take a nonjudgmental stance.

☐ Avoid shaming yourself and others.

☐ Avoid blaming yourself and others.

☐ Let go and let God.

☐ Non-striving.

☐ Yield to Life.

☐ Yield to Peace.

☐ Yield to Joy.

☐ Trust and surrender.

☐ Commit to your practice.

XVI. other useful concepts

♦ You are here with others to catalyze one another's **awakenings**.

♦ All the circumstances that befall you are serving **the needs of your soul**. Everything that occurs to you can offer you insight, which in turn can be used for growth and learning to fulfill your destiny.

♦ Keep in the forefront that every belief, perception, thought form, and attitude serves as a '**lens**' through which you view and experience reality. In other words, **your thinking creates your reality.**

♦ By **accepting** what is, you enhance your awareness of your reality. The more you accept all the different aspects of your reality (your thoughts, feelings, experiences), the more you will become **tuned in** to yourself and to the world around you.

♦ Acceptance does not mean you have to **like** what is happening.

♦ Imagine yourself **breathing in** the qualities that you want to experience more of: peace, love, serenity, joy, courage, kindness, compassion, understanding, empathy.

♦ **Guidance** is continuously being offered. To hear, you have only to listen. Guidance is only a prayer away.

♦ When you attempt to tune out your awareness (through addictions), you are, in effect, **abandoning yourself and your connection with divine guidance**.

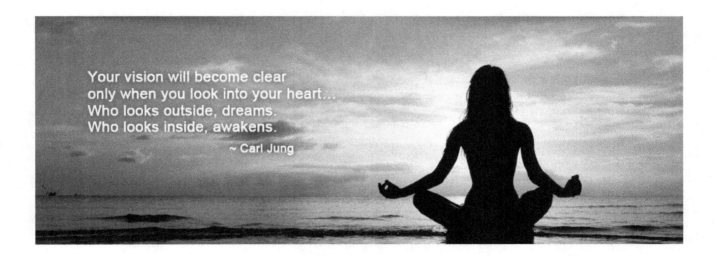

Your vision will become clear
only when you look into your heart...
Who looks outside, dreams.
Who looks inside, awakens.
~ Carl Jung

Editor's note: Chapters 8 and 10 of this book contain material that was abridged and adapted from *Living in Alignment: a Practical Guide to Personal Transformation* by Darcy S. Clarke (2012), available from **www.Amazon.com** in print or as a Kindle E-book.

To learn more about the Living in Alignment Program, please purchase the *Guide* or explore **www.LivingInAlignment.ca** and join the author's email list.

personal notes:

recommended reading

Codependence

- *Adult Children of Abusive Parents* Steven Farmer, MA, MFCC
- *An Adult Child's Guide To What Is Normal* John Friel, PhD and Linda Friel, MA
- *Beyond Codependency, and Getting Better All the Time* Melody Beattie
- *Boundaries: Where You End and I Begin* Anne Katherine, MA
- *Breaking Free* Pia Mellody, RN
- *Breaking Free of the Codependency Trap* Barry and Janae Weinhold
- *Codependent No More: How to Stop Controlling Others and Start Caring For Yourself* Melody Beattie
- *Codependence, the Dance of Wounded Souls: A cosmic perspective of codependence and the human condition* Robert Burney
- *Compelled To Control* J. Keith Miller
- *Do I Have to Give Up Me To Be Loved By God?* Margaret Paul, PhD
- *Facing Codependence* Pia Mellody, RN
- *Gentle Reminders, Daily Affirmations for Codependents* Mitzi Chandler
- *Healing The Child Within* Charles L. Whitfield
- *Healing the Wounds of Codependence: a Guide to Reclaiming Your Life* Darcy S. Clarke
- *Home Coming, Reclaiming And Championing Your Inner Child* John Bradshaw
- *Love Is A Choice* Dr. Robert Hemfelt, Dr. Frank Minirth and Dr. Paul Meier, MD
- *The Addictive Organization* Anne Wilson Schaef and Diane Fassel
- *The Chalice and the Blade* Riane Eisler
- *The Enabler, When Helping Harms The Ones You Love* Angelyn Miller
- *The Intimacy Factor* Pia Mellody, RN and Lawrence S. Freundlich
- *Toxic Parents, Overcoming their Hurtful Legacy and Reclaiming Your Life* Dr. Susan Forward
- *Trapped in the Mirror, Adult Children of Narcissists in their Struggle for Self* Elan Golomb, PhD
- *Why Your Life Sucks and What You Can Do About It* Alan H. Cohen

Abuse

- *Abused Boys, The Neglected Victims of Sexual Abuse* Mic Hunter
- *The Anger Guide* Claudia Black, PhD
- *The Battered Women* Lonore E. Walker
- *The Courage To Heal, A Guide For Women Survivors of Sexual Abuse* Ellen Bass and Laura Davis
- *The Verbally Abusive Relationship, How To Recognize It and How To Respond* Patricia Evans
- *Verbal Abuse, Survivors Speak Out On Relationships and Recovery* Patricia Evans
- *Victims No Longer, Men Recovering From Incest and Other Sexual Child Abuse* Mike Lew
- *Women Who Hurt Themselves* Dusty Miller

Addiction & Recovery

- *A Hole in the Sidewalk* Claudia Black, PhD
- *Accepting Ourselves and Others, A Journey Into Recovery From Addictive and Compulsive Behaviors For Gays, Lesbians and Bisexuals* Sheppard B. Kominars, PhD and Kathryn D. Kominars, PhD
- *Addiction and Grace* Gerald G May, MD
- *Addiction-Free Pain Management: Relapse Prevention Counseling Workbook* Stephen F. Grinstead and Terence T. Gorski
- *Bradshaw On: Healing The Shame That Binds You* John Bradshaw
- *Changing Course* Claudia Black, PhD
- *Coming Out Of Shame, Transforming Gay and Lesbian Lives* Gershen Kaufman, PhD and Lev Raphael, PhD
- *Cybersex Unhooked, A Workbook for Breaking Free of Compulsive Online Sexual Behavior* David L. Delmonico, PhD, Elizabeth Griffin, MA, Joseph Moriarity
- *Disclosing Secrets: an Addict's Guide for When, To Whom, and How Much To Reveal* M. Deborah Corley PhD and Jennifer P. Schneider MD
- *Facing the Shadow* Patrick J. Carnes, PhD
- *Family Secrets - The Path To Self Acceptance and Reunion* John Bradshaw
- *Good Grief* Granger E. Westberg
- *It Will Never Happen To Me!* Claudia Black, PhD
- *It's Never To Late To Have A Happy Childhood* Claudia Black, PhD
- *Learning To Love Yourself, Finding Your Self Worth* Sharon Wegscheider-Cruse
- *Letting Go Of Shame: Understanding How Shame Affects Your Life* Ronald Potter-Efron and Patricia Potter-Efron
- *Love Is Letting Go of Fear* Gerald G. Jampolsky, MD
- *Mind Over Mood: Change How You Feel by Changing the Way You Think* Dennis Greenberger, PhD, Christine A. Padesky, PhD
- *No Ordinary Moments: A Peaceful Warrior's Guide to Daily Life* Dan Millman
- *Passages Through Recovery, An Action Plan For Preventing Relapse* Terence T. Gorski
- *Relapse Toolkit* Claudia Black, PhD
- *Repeat After Me* Claudia Black, PhD
- *Self Esteem, A Family Affair* Jean Illsely Clarke
- *Shame And Guilt: The Masters of Disguise* Jane Middelton-Moz
- *Stage II Relationships: Love Beyond Addiction* Earnie Larsen
- Succulent *Wild Woman* Sark
- *Taking Responsibility* Nathaniel Branden, PhD
- *The Addictive Personality: Understanding The Addictive Process and Compulsive Behavior* (2nd ed.) Craig Nakken
- *The Artist's Way: A Spiritual Path to Higher Creativity* Julia Cameron
- *The Betrayal Bond: Breaking Free of Exploitive Relationships* Patrick J. Carnes, PhD
- *The Creative Journal: The Art of Finding Yourself* Lucia Capacchione, PhD, ATR
- *The Emotional Incest Syndrome* Dr. Patricia Love
- *The Greatest Miracle In The World* Og Mandino
- *The Language Of Letting Go* Melody Beattie

- *The Power of Two: Secrets to a Strong & Loving Marriage* Susan Heitler, PhD
- *The Primal Wound: Understanding the Adopted Child* Nancy Newton Verrier
- The Return of the Ragpicker Og Mandino
- *The Staying Sober Workbook* Terence T. Gorski
- *Today I Feel Silly and Other Moods That Make My Day* Jamie Lee Curtis
- *Twelve Jewish Steps To Recovery* Rabbi Kerry M. Olitzky and Stuart A Copans, MD
- *Way Of The Peaceful Warrior* Dan Millman
- *Workaholics, The Respectable Addicts* Barbara Killinger, PhD

Alcohol/Drug Addiction

- *A Hole in the Sidewalk* Claudia Black, PhD
- *Addictive Thinking: Understanding Self-Deception* Abraham J. Twerski, MD
- *Adult Children of Alcoholics* Janet Geringer Woititz
- *Alcoholics Anonymous* Alcoholics Anonymous
- *Bradshaw On: Healing The Shame That Binds You* John Bradshaw
- *From Survival To Recovery: Growing Up In An Alcoholic Home* Al-Anon Family Groups
- *Getting Love Right: Learning The Choices Of Healthy Intimacy* Terence T. Gorski
- *I'll Quit Tomorrow A Practical Guide to Alcoholism Treatment* Vernon E. Johnson
- *Living Sober* Alcoholics Anonymous World Services
- *My Dad Loves Me, My Dad Has a Disease* Claudia Black, PhD
- *Of Course You're Angry, A Guide To Dealing With The Emotions of Substance Abuse* Gayle Rosellini and Mark Worden
- *Staying Sober* Terence T. Gorski and Merlene Miller
- *Stepping Stones To Recovery From Cocaine/Crack Addiction* James Jennings
- *The Courage To Change* Dennis Wholey
- *The Staying Sober Workbook* Terence T. Gorski
- *Twelve Steps and Twelve Traditions* Alcholics Anonymous World Services
- *Under the Influence, A Guide to the Myths and Realities of Alcoholism* Dr. James R. Milam and Katherine Ketcham

Love Addiction

- *Facing Love Addiction* Pia Mellody, RN
- *Leaving the Enchanted Forest* Stephanine Covington and Liana Beckett
- *Sex and Love Addicts Anonymous* Sex and Love Addicts Anonymous
- *Women, Sex and Addiction* Charlotte Davis Kasl, PhD

Sex Addiction

- *A Gentle Path Through the Twelve Steps* Patrick J. Carnes, PhD
- *A Hole in the Sidewalk* Claudia Black, PhD
- *Contrary to Love* Patrick J. Carnes, PhD
- *Cybersex Unhooked, A Workbook for Breaking Free of Compulsive Online Sexual Behavior* David L. Delmonico, PhD, Elizabeth Griffin, MA, Joseph Moriarity

- *Don't Call It Love* Patrick J. Carnes, PhD
- *Facing the Shadow* Patrick J. Carnes, PhD
- *Hope And Recovery, A Twelve Step Guide for Healing From Compulsive Sexual Behavior* Anonymous
- *In The Shadows Of The Net Breaking Free of Compulsive Online Sexual Behavior* Patrick J. Carnes PhD, David Delmonico PhD, Elizabeth Griffin, MA
- *No Stones: Women Redeemed from Sexual Addiction* Marnie C. Ferree and Mark Laaser
- *Open Hearts - Renewing Relationships with Recovery, Romance & Reality* Patrick J. Carnes, PhD
- *Out Of the Shadows* Patrick J. Carnes, PhD
- *Sexaholics Anonymous*
- *Sexual Anorexia* Patrick J. Carnes, PhD with Joseph M. Moriarity
- *Silently Seduced, When Parents Make Children Partners* Kenneth M. Adams, PhD

Other Addictions

- *Addictive Thinking: Understanding Self-Deception* Abraham J. Twerski, MD
- *Brain Lock* Jeffrey M. Schwartz, MD
- *Chained to the Desk: A Guidebook For Workaholics, Their Partners and Children, and the Clinicians Who Treat Them* Bryan E. Robinson, PhD
- *How To Get Out of Debt, Stay Out of Debt and Live Prosperously* Jerrold Mundis
- *I Hate You, Don't Leave Me* Jerold J. Kreisman, MD and Hal Straus
- *Money Drunk, Money Sober, 90 Days To Financial Freedom* Julia Cameron and Mark Bryan
- *Too Perfect: When Being In Control Gets Out of Control* Allan E. Mallinger, MD and Jeannette DeWyze
- *Workaholics, The Respectable Addicts* Barbara Killinger, PhD
- *Working Ourselves To Death: the High Cost of Workaholism and the Rewards of Recovery* Diane Fassel

12 Steps

- *A Gentle Path Through the Twelve Steps* Patrick J. Carnes, PhD
- *A Woman's Way through the Twelve Steps* Stephanie S. Covington, PhD
- *Alcoholics Anonymous* Alcoholics Anonymous
- *Facing Love Addiction* Pia Mellody, RN
- *Getting Love Right: Learning the Choices of Healthy Intimacy* Terence T. Gorski
- *Relapse Toolkit* Claudia Black, PhD
- *The 12 Steps for Adult Children*
- *The Dual Disorders Recovery Book*
- *The Twelve Steps and Dual Disorders* Tim Hamilton and Pat Samples
- *The Twelve Steps For Christians Based on Biblical Teachings*
- *Twelve Jewish Steps To Recovery* Rabbi Kerry M. Olitzky and Stuart A. Copans, MD
- *Twelve Steps and Twelve Traditions* Alcoholics Anonymous World Services

Family Issues

- *Adult Children, the Secrets of Dysfunctional Families* John Friel and Linda Friel
- *Always Daddy's Girl* H. Norman Wright
- *Before You Forget* Kelly DuMar
- *Bradshaw On: The Family* John Bradshaw
- *Children of Trauma, Rediscovering Your Discarded Self* Jane Middelton - Moz
- *Coming Out, an Act of Love* Rob Eichberg, PhD
- *Daily Affirmations for Parents* Tian Dayton, PhD
- *Facing Shame* Merle A. Fossum and Marilyn Mason
- *Freeing Our Families from Perfection* Thomas S. Greenspon, PhD
- *Growing Up Again, Parenting Ourselves, Parenting Our Children* Jean Illsley Clarke and Connie Dawson
- *How to Talk So Kids Will Listen & Listen So Kids Will Talk* Adele Faber and Elaine Mazlish
- *It Will Never Happen To Me!* Claudia Black, PhD
- *Longing For Dad, Father Loss and Its Impact* Beth M. Erickson, PhD
- *Love You Forever* Robert Munsch
- *My Dad Loves Me, My Dad Has a Disease* Claudia Black, PhD
- *My Mother My Self, the Daughter's Search For Self* Nancy Friday
- *Self Esteem, A Family Affair* Jean Illsely Clarke
- *Shame And Guilt: The Masters of Disguise* Jane Middelton-Moz
- *Silently Seduced, When Parents Make Children Partners* Kenneth M Adams, PhD
- *The Birth Order Book* Dr. Kevin Leman
- *The Drama of the Gifted Child* Alice Miller
- *The Emotional Incest Syndrome* Dr. Patricia Love
- *The Worst Loss* Barbara D. Rosof

Relationships

- *After the Affair: Healing the Pain and Rebuilding Trust When a Partner Has Been Unfaithful* Janis Abrahms Spring, PhD
- *Awakening Your Sexuality: A Guide for Recovering Women* Stephanie S. Covington, PhD
- *Boundaries and Relationships* Charles L. Whitfield, MD
- *Creating Love, The Next Stage of Growth* John Bradshaw
- *Do I Have To Give Up Me To Be Loved By God?* Margaret Paul, PhD
- *Facing Love Addiction* Pia Mellody, RN
- *Getting the Love You Want* Harvill Hendrix, PhD
- *Healing For Damaged Emotions Workbook* David A. Seamands and Beth Funk
- *Heartwounds, The Impact of Unresolved Trauma and Grief On Relationships* Tian Dayton, PhD
- *How Can I get Through to You?* Terrence Real
- *I Love You Enough To . . . Let You Go* Jim McGregor
- *If Only He Knew, Understanding Your Wife* Gary Smalley
- *If the Buddha Dated: a Handbook for Finding Love on a Spiritual Path* Charlotte Davis Kasl, PhD
- *Is It Love Or Is It Addiction* Brenda Schaefer
- *Keeping The Love You Find* Harville Hendrix, PhD

Reading

- *Open Hearts - Renewing Relationships with Recovery, Romance & Reality* Patrick J. Carnes, PhD
- *The Anger Guide* Claudia Black, PhD
- *The Birth Order Book* Dr. Kevin Leman
- *The Dance of Intimacy: A Woman's Guide to Courageous Acts of Change in Key Relationships* Harriet Lerner, PhD
- *The Intimacy Factor* Pia Mellody, RN and Lawrence S. Freundlich
- *The Knight In Rusty Armor* Robert Fisher
- *The Missing Piece* Shel Silverstein
- *The Princess Who Believed in Fairy Tales* Marcia Grad
- *The Verbally Abusive Relationship, How to Recognize It and How to Respond* Patricia Evans
- *Undefended Love* Jett Psaris and Marlena Tyons
- *Verbal Abuse: Survivors Speak Out On Relationships and Recovery* Patricia Evans
- *Why Am I Afraid To Love? Overcoming Rejection and Indifference* John Powell, SJ
- *Why Am I Afraid To Tell You Who I Am? Insights into Personal Growth* John Powell, SJ
- *You Just Don't Understand, Women and Men In Conversation* Deborah Tannen, PhD

Emotions

- *A Journey Through Grief* Alla Renée Bozarth, PhD
- *A Path With Heart* Jack Kornfield
- *Dare To Be Yourself: How to Quit Being an Extra in Other People's Movies and Become the Star of Your Own* Alan Cohen
- *Feel The Fear and Do It Anyway* Susan Jeffers, PhD
- *Feelings Buried Alive Never Die* Karol K. Truman
- *Gathering Peace: A Journey of Discovery* Peggy Warren
- *How Can I get Through to You?* Terrence Real
- *I Don't Want To Talk About It* Terrence Real
- *Love Is Letting Go Of Fear* Gerald G. Jampolsky, MD
- *Of Course You're Angry, a Guide to Dealing With the Emotions of Substance Abuse* Gayle Rosellini and Mark Worden
- *Shame and Guilt: The Masters of Disguise* Jane Middelton-Moz
- *The Creative Journal: The Art of Finding Yourself* Lucia Capacchione, PhD, ATR
- *The Intimacy Factor* Pia Mellody, RN and Lawrence S. Freundlich
- *The Missing Piece* Shel Silverstein

Inspiration

- *A Deep Breath Of Life: Daily Inspiration For Heart-Centered Living* Alan Cohen
- *A Journey Through Grief* Alla Renée Bozarth, PhD
- *Believing In Myself: Daily Meditations for Healing and Building Self-Esteem* Earnie Larsen and Carol Hegarty
- *Dare To Be Yourself: How to Quit Being an Extra in Other People's Movies and Become the Star of Your Own* Alan Cohen
- *Gathering Peace: A Journey of Discovery* Peggy Warren
- *Getting Love Right: Learning the Choices of Healthy Intimacy* Terence T. Gorski

- *Handle with Prayer: Harnessing the Power to Make Your Dreams Come Through* Alan Cohen
- *How Good Do We Have To Be? A New Understanding of Guilt and Forgiveness* Harold S. Kushner
- *Kitchen Table Wisdom: Stories That Heal* Rachel Naomi Remen, MD
- *Night Light: a Book of Nighttime Meditations* Amy E. Dean
- *One Day My Soul Just Opened Up* Iyanla Vanzant
- *Sacred Journey of the Peaceful Warrior* Dan Millman
- *The Giving Tree* Shel Silverstein
- *The Healing Drum* Blackwolf Jones, MS, CAS and Gina Jones
- *When Bad Things Happen To Good People* Harold Kushner
- *Why Your Life Sucks and What You Can Do About It* Alan H. Cohen

Meditation/Relaxation

- *A Cherokee Feast of Days: Daily Meditations* Joyce Sequichie Hifler
- *A Path With Heart* Jack Kornfield
- *A Woman's Spirit, More Meditations For Women* Hazelton Foundation
- *Acts of Faith: Daily Meditations for People of Color* Iyanla Vanzant
- *Affirmations For The Inner Child* Rokelle Lerner
- *Answers In The Heart, Daily Meditations* Hazelden Meditation Series
- *Around The Year With Emmet Fox, A Book of Daily Readings* Emmet Fox
- *Awakening: Conversations with the Master* Anthony de Mello, SJ
- *Believing In Myself: Daily Meditations for Healing and Building Self-Esteem* Earnie Larsen and Carol Hegarty
- *Daily Affirmations for Parents* Tian Dayton, PhD
- *Daily Affirmations For Adult Children of Alcoholics* Rokelle Lerner
- *Day by Day: Daily Meditations For Recovering Addicts* Anonymous
- *Each Day A New Beginning, Daily Meditations For Women* Karen Casey
- *Gathering Peace: A Journey of Discovery* Peggy Warren
- *Gentle Reminders, Daily Affirmations for Codependents* Mitzi Chandler
- *Glad Day: Daily Meditations For Gay, Lesbian, Bisexual & Transgender People* Joan Larkin
- *In God's Care, Daily Meditations on Spirituality In Recovery* Karen Casey
- *Journey To The Heart, Daily Meditations On The Path To Freeing Your Soul* Melody Beattie
- *Meditations For Men Who Do Too Much* Jonathon Lazear
- *Meditations For Women Who Do Too Much* Anne Wilson Schaef
- *Search for Serenity and How to Achieve It* Lewis F. Presnall
- *The Language of Letting Go* Melody Beattie
- *Touchstones, A Book of Daily Meditations For Men* A Hazelden Book
- *Yesterday's Tomorrow: Recovery Meditations For Hard Cases* Barry Longyear

Spirituality

- *A Deep Breath Of Life: Daily Inspiration For Heart-Centered Living* Alan Cohen
- *A Path With Heart* Jack Kornfield
- *A Return to Love* Marianne Williamson
- *Acts of Faith: Daily Meditations for People of Color* Iyanla Vanzant
- *Addiction and Grace* Gerald G May, MD
- *Awakening: Conversations with the Master* Anthony de Mello, SJ
- *Awareness: the Perils and Opportunities of Reality* Anthony de Mello, SJ
- *Do I Have To Give Up Me To Be Loved By God?* Margaret Paul, PhD
- *Earth Dance Drum: A Celebration of Life* Blackwolf Jones, MS, CAS and Gina Jones
- *Finding Your Way Home* Melody Beattie
- *God On A Harley* Joan Brady
- *Good Goats: Healing Our Image Of God* Dennis Linn, Sheila Fabricant Linn and Matthew Linn
- *Handle with Prayer: Harnessing the Power to Make Your Dreams Come Through* Alan Cohen
- *Illuminata, A Return To Prayer* Marianne Williamson
- *Kitchen Table Wisdom: Stories That Heal* Rachel Naomi Remen, MD
- *Let Me Grieve But Not Forever* Verdell Davis
- *Living in Alignment: a Practical Guide to Personal Transformation* Darcy S. Clarke
- *Living in Process: Basic Truths for Living the Path* Anne Wilson Schaef
- *One Day My Soul Just Opened Up* Iyanla Vanzant
- *Practicing the Power of Now* Eckhart Tolle
- *Prayers for a Planetary Pilgrim* Edward Hays
- *Rising to the Call* Jacquelyn Small and Mary Yovino
- Seven Arrows Hyemeyohsts Storm
- *Spiritual Literacy* Frederic and Mary Ann Brussat
- *The Artist's Way: a Spiritual Path to Higher Creativity* Julia Cameron
- *The Four Agreements* Don Miguel Ruiz
- *The Grief Recovery Handbook* John W. James and Russell Friedman
- *The Hero with a Thousand Faces* Joseph Campbell
- *The Inner Voice* Henri J. M. Nouwen
- *The Leader as Martial Artist* Arnold Mindell
- *The Observing Self: Mysticism and Psychotherapy* Arthur J. Deikman, MD
- *The Precious Present* Spencer Johnson
- *The Sermon on the Mount* Emmet Fox
- *Why Am I Afraid To Love? Overcoming Rejection and Indifference* John Powell, SJ
- *Why Am I Afraid To Tell You Who I Am? Insights into Personal Growth* John Powell, SJ

Other

- *The Warrior's Journey Home: Healing Men, Healing the Planet* Jed Diamond
- *The Money Trap* Ron Gallen

9 780991 710140